You can Write a Column

Monica McCabe Cardoza

WRITER'S DIGEST BOOKS
CINCINNATI, OHIO
www.writersdigest.com

You Can Write a Column. Copyright © 2000 by Monica McCabe Cardoza. Manufactured in the United States of America. All rights reserved. No part of this book may be reproduced in any form or by any electronic or mechanical means including information storage and retrieval systems without permission in writing from the publisher, except by a reviewer, who may quote brief passages in a review. Published by Writer's Digest Books, an imprint of F + W Publications, Inc., 4700 East Galbraith Road, Cincinnati, Ohio 45236. (800) 289-0963. First edition.

Visit our Web site at www.writersdigest.com for information on more resources for writers.

To receive a free weekly e-mail newsletter delivering tips and updates about writing and about Writer's Digest products, send an e-mail with "Subscribe Newsletter" in the body of the message to newsletter-request@writersdigest.com, or register directly at our Web site at www.writersdigest.com.

08   07   06   05   04   6   5   4   3   2

Library of Congress Cataloging-in-Publication Data

McCabe-Cardoza, Monica
    You can write a column / by Monica McCabe Cardoza.
      p.   cm.
    Includes index.
    ISBN 0-89879-924-4 (pbk.: alk. paper)
      1. Journalism—Authorship. 2. Newspapers—Sections, columns, etc. I. Title.

PN4784.C65 M38   2000
808'.06607—dc21   00-025597
                                                              CIP

Editors: Bob Beckstead and Meg Leder
Cover designer: Lisa Buchanan
Cover photography by: Al Parrish
Author photo by: David Cardoza
Production coordinator: Kristin D. Heller

For Max, whose honesty, humor and knowledge made
my first job editing columns my most memorable.

ACKNOWLEDGMENTS

From my first job editing columns for worldwide distribution to my current position writing and acquiring columns for a business trade magazine, I am constantly reminded of the special qualities inherent in columnists—specifically, their accessibility, willingness to share their experiences, passion for their craft and most importantly, their sense of humor. It's qualities such as these that have made writing this book a labor of love.

That said, I would like to thank the following people: *Working Wounded* columnist Bob Rosner; *Ask the Builder* columnist Tim Carter; *The Wild Side* columnist Dr. Scott Shalaway; *The Mature Traveler* columnists Gene Malott and Adele Malott; *Dona's Kitchen Kapers* columnist Dona Z. Meilach; humor columnist Larry Litt; self-syndicated columnist Azriela Jaffe; Dave Lieber of the National Society of Newspaper Columnists; Jim Toler of Toler Media Services; and Liz Parker of the Recorder Community Newspapers.

These people generously shared their experiences and opinions so that aspiring columnists could attain their goals. It is my hope that readers will use the information in these pages to find their unique voice and style and to realize the immense satisfaction that comes from column writing.

ABOUT THE AUTHOR

 As an editor with The New York Times Syndication Sales Corporation, Monica McCabe Cardoza edited hundreds of columns—on topics ranging from entertainment to home technology to relationships. Later, as an editor with a community newspaper, McCabe Cardoza wrote the paper's social column. Today, as an editor with a national business trade association, she edits columns, acquires new columns and writes an environmental column for its quarterly magazine.

McCabe Cardoza holds a bachelor's degree in journalism from New York University and a master's degree in publishing from Pace University. She is the author of *A Woman's Guide to Martial Arts: How to Choose a Discipline and Get Started* (The Overlook Press, 1996).

TABLE OF CONTENTS

PART ONE

Before Beginning

1 Why Write a Column?............................... 3

Whether it's for additional income, prestige or enjoyment, knowing why you want to write a column enables you to set strategies for attaining your goals.

2 What Type of Column Do You Want to Write? 15

From inspirational to instructional, discover the many types of columns and which format best matches your subject.

3 Get to Know the Markets 27

The market for columns is more diverse than ever, offering you a unique opportunity to find just the right home for your column.

4 Research Before You Write 38

Discover how to customize the subject and format of your column to complement the publication you've targeted.

PART TWO

Writing the Column

5 Getting Ideas 49

Learn to look for ideas in all the right places and read how successful columnists generate their own ideas.

PART THREE

Selling the Column

Since entering the world of publishing some fifteen years ago, I've written columns, hired columnists and edited well over a thousand columns—many of which have appeared in newspapers and magazines throughout the world.

Over the years, the market for columns has changed dramatically. But one thing hasn't changed: Publishers are constantly on the lookout for new columnists.

You Can Write a Column offers you an insider's view into the world of column writing. With clear, practical writing instruction and savvy marketing advice, it will answer all your questions about this exciting field.

Toward that goal, here's what you'll find:

- Before You Begin Writing:
    Locate the best markets for your column, including the expanding online market
    Discover the traits of successful columnists
    Learn what editors look for in a columnist
    Target the publications that want your work
- Dive Into the Nuts and Bolts of Writing:
    Generate ideas, and shape those ideas into finished columns
    Structure your column to appeal to editors
    Avoid common mistakes made by new columnists
    Find your unique "voice" and "style"
    Engage your audience, and keep them coming back
- Sell Your Column:
    Build a name for yourself as an expert
    Submit your work to a publication
    Continually market it to higher-paying publications
    Place your column in more than one publication

Invaluable exercises throughout this book will help you expand your range of topics and ideas. You'll also find valuable insight from successful columnists. Learn how they broke into their markets, developed their unique styles and turned column-writing into a financially rewarding full-time career. What worked for them can work for you.

PART ONE

Before Beginning

1 Why Write a Column?

Reading a well-crafted column is like being temporarily transported to another dimension. A travel column can whisk its readers off to the destination being described. A recipe column can make readers' mouths water. A humor column can cause readers to laugh aloud.

Columns can have this effect because the columnist's character is so firmly entrenched in the writing—to the point where it's difficult to separate columnists from their work. Former columnist Sam Riley summed it up this way: "The heart of journalism may be news reporting, and the soul of journalism the editorial page, but the personality of journalism is the column."

It's that ability to put so much of oneself into a column that makes column writing such an enormously rewarding form of expression. Certainly, it's difficult to think of an occupation more fulfilling than one that allows you to spend time with a subject about which you're passionate and explore it in all its intricacies.

But something as simple as a column can become quite complex when you begin to dissect it into its parts. You quickly realize that a great deal of work has gone into those few hundred words.

Before a columnist can get published, he has to find a subject niche—something specific about which to write, but not so specific as to narrow the potential audience and topics of the column. He has to find out whether other columnists are writing on the same subject and study their work to see how his differs from theirs. Then he has to outline topic ideas and flesh out at least several finished columns to show editors. To sell the idea to an editor, he has to position himself as the right person for the job.

Once the column is published, he must continually think about the next topic, striving to make every one better. Indeed, just as actors are only as good as their last movie, columnists are only as good as their last column.

Sounds like a lot of work. But columnists know it's worth it. They thrive on the opportunity to outperform on every column. They welcome the challenge of generating ideas, then compiling them into cohesive, well-organized, exciting columns that draw in readers.

Columnists are driven by the personal, and sometimes financial, satisfaction that comes from seeing their thoughts and ideas in print on a regular basis. Indeed, column writing is an enormously rewarding occupation, and one that is worth every drop of sweat when you're finally published.

A Close-Up View

In 1983, I graduated from New York University with a degree in journalism and consequently landed my first editorial job at The New York Times Syndication Sales Corporation, a newspaper syndicate that sells articles and columns to newspapers and magazines around the world. Part of my job involved editing columns.

As a column editor, I got a close-up view of what it takes to be a columnist. During my six years there, I edited all sorts of columns—advice, rock music, celebrity, television, commentary, military and home technology columns. I probably edited more than fifteen hundred columns during that time.

But it wasn't until I became a columnist myself that I gained a true appreciation of the column-writing craft. Suddenly, I was the one responsible for developing ideas and fleshing them out into final form. I learned how to put new spins on topics I'd covered hundreds of times. I got to the point where I could almost write a column to the exact word count required by my editor—without the use of my computer's "word count" function.

During my time at the "syndicate," I worked closely with Leo Buscaglia, whose *Living and Loving* column rarely failed to touch readers' hearts. Though he wrote on the broad topic of "love," he continually found fresh approaches to that age-old subject, and he did so in a sincere way. In fact, he was such a loving person that he would give you a great big bear hug every time he saw you.

Reasons to Write a Column

Columnists, such as Leo Buscaglia, whose work is carried by many publications—often on a worldwide basis—can do well financially. While few columnists realize those kinds of rewards early in their column-writing careers, many aren't writing columns for those reasons. I've worked with people who write their columns for free, others who request a small fee to cover expenses and still others who expect three-figure payments for each column.

Indeed, in my fifteen years of working with columnists and being a columnist, I'd have to say that there is usually no one single reason why people pursue column writing. Personal and professional reasons often overlap. Whether you're a human resources manager looking to use your column to jump-start your own business or a hobbyist seeking to sell more copies of your book covering the hobby you study, you'll probably have more than one goal you wish to achieve through your columns.

Some people aspire to become columnists simply to see their names in print. For them, the thrill of being published and receiving credit for their work is immensely satisfying.

Others enjoy writing for a small publication that allows them to be a big fish in a small pond. Open your community newspaper and note the columns written by local residents. Perhaps there's a photo of the columnist that runs next to the column's text. The columnist's name, known as a byline, probably runs in large type near the photo. Chances are that person is recognized in public by members of the community and may also be asked to speak at community functions, such as dedications and awards ceremonies.

Some aspiring columnists simply want to share their thoughts and ideas with others. Perhaps you've researched the history of your area and want to share what you've learned. Or maybe you have a knack for capturing in words the feelings and experiences of members of your community, and you enjoy the act of putting those words on paper for all to read.

Perhaps in addition to writing a column for the reasons already cited you want to enhance your professional status. If you've written a book, consider using it as the basis for a column. Writing a column on the topic of your book might increase sales of the book and build on your reputation as an expert in the field.

On the other hand, maybe you want to write a book on a particular topic. A column could get you started. The column could form the basis of the book or it could be the book itself. Once you have twenty or thirty published columns under your belt, a book publisher might be interested in compiling them into a book. Such books are common. A word search for "columnists" on an online bookstore turned up almost four hundred books by columnists—everything from humor columnist Dave Barry to advice columnist Ann Landers, with lots of books by less well-known authors in between.

Maybe you work in an industry that has been financially good to you, and you want to give back some of what you were given. Writing a column for the association magazine that covers your industry could be one way of doing that. Or maybe you see your association magazine as a vehicle for putting your name before your peers.'

Perhaps you already earn your living as a writer—whether as a free-lancer or as a full-time writer in public relations or corporate communications. You might parlay your writing skills into your dream job with a particular magazine or newspaper. Breaking in as a columnist could be your ticket to a full-time job with that publication.

Opportunity May Already Be Knocking

If there is only one lesson you walk away with after reading this book—although I hope you walk away with lots more—it's that you should never underestimate your potential as a columnist. Breaking into column writing can be tough. In fact, it can be as much work, or more, as writing the columns themselves. But sometimes opportunity is there, just waiting for you to grab hold of it.

The first column I wrote was offered to me out of the blue. I had never before written a column and had only one previously published article to my name. I couldn't even claim expertise in the topic of the column I was being offered to write.

At the time, I worked as a reporter and salesperson for a community newspaper. One day, the publisher of the paper asked me if I wanted to write a social column. However, since my byline already appeared in the paper, he wanted the column to be written under a pseudonym. The material for the column—birth announcements, marriages, birthdays, vacations and the like—would be gathered during my sales calls to local business people. The publisher's intention was to flatter potential advertisers by publishing their news in the paper, then getting their business.

Though I was paid just twenty-five dollars per column, considering the year was 1990 and I was just starting out as a writer, the pay wasn't too bad. According to the 2000 *Writer's Market*, newspapers pay forty dollars and up for local columns.

My second experience as a columnist was an opportunity that also basically fell into my lap. As an editor at a trade association, I was responsible for covering the environmental regulations affecting our members, which were printing companies. Attending conferences, seminars and meetings on this topic, I quickly became the in-house expert and was consequently asked to write a column for the association's quarterly magazine.

There are many people out there who are capable of writing a column and who would be welcome with open arms by editors looking to cover a topic on a regular basis. Look at what you do for a living and consider whether you could turn your expertise into a column.

Establish Goals

By establishing goals related to column writing, you may be able to parlay your experience into a column in a mainstream magazine or a syndicated commentary column. By thinking about what you want to achieve, you can begin to set goals and implement strategies for achieving them.

Fine-tuning your goal is one way to increase the chances of achieving it. Saying, "I want to be a columnist" is too vague. Saying, "I want to write an opinion column for my area's daily newspaper" is better, but not quite there yet.

There are many well-established opinion columnists, and chances are your area's daily paper already has one or more. You need to differentiate yourself from other opinion columnists and even question whether there are other types of columns you are better suited to writing. Ask yourself such specific questions as, Should I write a profile column focusing on people in my area instead of an opinion column? Is there enough material for me to generate a weekly column, or should I limit myself to a twice-a-month format? Would I settle for starting at my local weekly newspaper? Would I work for free to get into the column-writing business?

Now state your revised goal based on the questions you've asked yourself. You might say, "I want to write a twice-a-month column for my local paper. My column will profile work-at-home parents and how they combine career with child-raising." This statement clearly articulates your goal and enables you to start realizing it sooner.

Exercise

It's your turn. Put your goal into one sentence. Fine-tune it to make it as specific as possible. Now determine how realistic it is to expect to attain this goal. By committing your goal to paper, you refine it, and by refining it, you begin to focus on what you have to do to achieve it.

Establish a realistic time frame for achieving your goal. Start by determining how much time you can devote to developing your column. It might take a year to develop ideas for your column, write sample columns and research where your column should run. By understanding that it could take as much as, or more than, a year to accomplish these tasks, you won't get discouraged after six months have passed and you have only three columns written.

Exercise

Draw a time line representing the amount of time you expect to take to achieve your goal. Divide the line into yearly, monthly or weekly increments, depending on the length of time you have chosen, and plot the steps you will take toward achieving your goal. These steps include, but are not limited to, developing a list of topics, researching appropriate periodicals for your work, writing sample columns and marketing your work. You now have a time line that will keep you motivated, on track and focused on one task at a time.

It generally took me a full working day—seven hours—to write the environmental column for the trade association magazine I mentioned previously. In fact, writing the column was the easy part.

Prior to writing it, I'd have to decide on a topic—say, a new safety regulation on protecting employees from loud noise generated by printing presses—make some calls to environmental consultants to ensure that the regulation did indeed affect printing companies and make additional calls to printers to see if they would agree to be interviewed on the topic. Then, I'd write a paragraph explaining the topic, how I would approach it and who I would interview. I'd submit that to my editor, who would in turn have to get approval for the idea from her supervisor. By the time I'd get approval to go with the topic, two weeks might pass.

Not all columnists go through this process. Established columnists often generate their own topics without having to get approval. But recognize that it is a reality for many columnists, especially new ones breaking into a publication.

Turn on the Creative Juices

You can draw inspiration for a column from many areas, including hobbies, careers and experiences. Within these areas are numerous subjects just waiting to be written about. Popular subjects today include New Age, spirituality, aging, religion, health and fitness, family leisure, computers, travel, fashion and cooking.

But just because a subject is popular, doesn't mean you can't break in. It just requires creativity—coming up with a unique angle or fresh approach.

Advice columnists have been around for years, but that hasn't stopped new columnists from entering the advice field. Amy Alkon positions her column, *Ask the Advice Goddess*, as a hipper counterpart to Ann Landers.

Magazines that carry columns covering popular subjects often have on-staff editors or a stable of contributing editors who write these columns. However, you can still break into these publications. Some offer freelance writers the opportunity to write columns based on the writer's outline or completed manuscript.

To find opportunities for freelancers at a particular publication, refer to the current *Writer's Market*, a yearly reference book containing editorial information on hundreds of publications, or contact the publication directly and request writer's guidelines—some publications mail their guidelines, while others post them on their Web sites. Writer's guidelines describe a magazine's purpose and audience and outline specifications for submitting material, including word counts, categories and topics needed and, sometimes, rates of pay.

Not all publications provide guidelines. For those that do, it's a tremendous way to gain insight into a publication. However, the unavailability of writer's guidelines is no indication of a publication's unwillingness to publish freelance work. So go ahead and pursue publications that don't issue guidelines.

Whether or not a publication issues guidelines, every aspiring columnist must review current and past issues of the publications they've targeted. In addition to reading them through cover to cover, you want to *study* them. Chapter four describes specific ways to do that.

You'll increase your chances of seeing your column published if you're willing to narrow its focus and start with a small publication, such as a community newspaper. With the growing interest in native species of plants, a gardening columnist writing about plant species native to a particular area might be greeted enthusiastically by a local newspaper or city or state magazine.

And just as everything old is new again, so too are columns. Many columns are based on tried-and-true formats, but they cover new subjects. Take commuter columns, which broke onto the scene about fifteen years ago as an outlet for drivers' road rage. Though the subject is fairly new, the format is not. An article in *Editor & Publisher* compared commuter columns to "Action Line" columns popular a decade or two ago. According to the article: "As with Action Line columns, government officials often rectify problems as soon as the columnist expresses a concern."

Or take society columns, which have been resurrected in many newspapers, but with a new twist. Long a fixture of many newspapers, the society column, also known as gossip column, often covered the antics of the upper crust. Today, few editors are likely to want to publish such a column in its traditional form.

The Trentonian newspaper, however, came up with a new version of the society column, which it calls a "democratic social column." The column covers fund-raisers and other social events of the Trenton and Princeton, New Jersey, areas. While it may sound hokey to cover CEOs at a charity golf outing or the mayor at an awards dinner, small weeklies and large metropolitan newspapers appreciate these columns for several reasons: They give members in a community the chance to have their names mentioned, which makes people feel important; and they give readers a feeling for the social life of the town in which they live. Haven't you ever found yourself reading such a column, looking for someone you recognize—even if it is only your doctor or lawyer?

Exercise

If the subject of your proposed column is popular, you can increase your chances of getting it published by putting a new twist on how the subject is covered. Do this by imagining how your subject will be covered five years from now.

If you need help, do a little research. *American Demographics* magazine, for example, tracks population trends and their effects on the marketplace and is often available at local libraries. Use your research to predict how your subject will change, then gear your column toward those changes. If your instincts prove right, editors will clamor for your work.

A way to break in with a popular subject is to be outspoken. One columnist was able to parlay his outspokenness into a column for three daily newspapers. The weekly column, *Only Human*, which began running in 1991, is written by the Reverend Michael Riley, who has discussed his vasectomy after the birth of his fourth son and expounded on adultery.

Though the column resulted in Riley losing more than one hundred parishioners of his Stelton Baptist Church in Edison Township, New Jersey, and complaints from newspaper readers, the editor of one of the papers rewarded Riley by hiring him as a full-time feature writer.

The lesson here is that if you can write on controversial topics in such a way as not to offend everyone, many editors will be pleased. Such a tactic generates publicity for the paper—and publicity, good or bad, is often preferred over no publicity.

If you don't wish to paint yourself as a controversial figure writing about a popular topic, then consider basing one of your columns on a controversial topic related to the subject of your column. For example, if you write a column on nutrition, you could cover the controversy that erupted following publication of *Baby and Child Care* by Dr. Benjamin Spock, which espoused a diet free of meat and dairy products for everyone over the age of two. You could address the issue and even ask your readers to write you with their opinions.

Here's What It Takes

Ready to make the leap to published columnist? Based on my experience, I've compiled a checklist of ten qualities that can help you achieve your goals.

1. *Effective columnists meet deadlines.* One of the best ways to get on an editor's good side is to meet deadlines. Your editor will tell you when to submit your column, but keep in mind that holidays and your editor's vacations and other time off may require that you submit work early.

    One way to avoid missing deadlines is to submit backup columns to be used for times when you can't write a column, such as when you're ill or are on vacation. Backup columns cover generic topics that are not tied to a holiday or event and can therefore be published at any time throughout the year. In my local newspaper, I noticed that the editor had to reprint a column that had run three months previously because the author was unable to submit a new column. Some editors might not be so generous and could decide to give the space to another writer.

2. *Effective columnists focus on narrow areas within a niche.* General topics are fine, but with so much information available, readers want

information specific to themselves. Find that small niche that isn't being covered, or is not being covered well, and you've got yourself a solid foundation from which to start your column-writing career.

3. *Effective columnists write fairly and accurately.* I probably would not have even included these qualities were it not for the recent controversies over a columnist who was found to have fabricated people and quotations in her columns and another columnist who failed to attribute material in his column to the original writer. The columnists worked at *The Boston Globe*, and the findings spurred the media to take a closer look at the fact-checking practices employed at various newspapers and magazines. Incidentally, the columnists were asked to resign, and both eventually did.

    Speaking at the 1999 National Society of Newspaper Columnists convention, *The Boston Globe* managing editor Greg Moore said the paper would devote more time and attention to editing columns, question columnists about their sources and give columnists three-year assignments (with possible renewals), rather than assuming they'll write their columns indefinitely. "The notion that you have a column and get to do it for twenty-five years is history at the *Globe*," he said.

    Whether you're writing a column based on your personal observations or your expertise in a particular area, keep copies of all the materials you used to write your column, including transcripts of interviews and copies of articles. If the editor says, "You mentioned the author of an obscure book, and I want to check the spelling of the author's name and the title of the book," you can produce the material and save the editor lots of valuable time.

4. *Effective columnists know their audiences.* The ability to know and understand the concerns and interests of a particular audience is key to becoming a successful columnist.

    One way to tap into your readers' concerns and interests is to learn about the audience via demographic information available from companies that publish advertising-related data on various media. For example, SRDS is a company that provides information on the readers of specific publications. (See the Resources section for contact information for SRDS.)

5. *Effective columnists go beyond demographic data and initiate discus-*

sions with their audiences. Encourage your readers to write to you, and if you receive a substantial amount of mail, make sure your editor knows it.

Also, try to answer all your mail. Gene and Adele Malott, authors of *The Mature Traveler* column, estimate they receive up to two hundred letters a month—and they answer them all. (For the complete interview with the Malotts, please see pages 112-113.)

One columnist went so far as to bring his readers together—literally. After about twenty-five readers E-mailed *Kansas City Star* columnist Bill Tammeus about a column on the controversy over President Clinton taking communion during his trip to South Africa, Tammeus put these correspondents together in an electronic discussion group.

6. *Effective columnists think ahead.* Can you write a New Year's-themed column in July? You may have to if the publication for which you write has a long lead time, meaning the editor needs the column in July even though it won't be published until December. That time frame may not apply to most publications, but it clearly illustrates the flexibility required of many columnists.

7. *Effective columnists are well-versed in the topic on which they're writing.* One of the nice things about being a columnist is that you don't necessarily need to have a degree or professional experience related to the area on which you're writing. If you were to take up hiking as a hobby, climbing mountains, exploring new hiking destinations and reading all you can on hiking may eventually qualify you as a pseudo-expert on the subject. Perhaps your local newspaper would welcome a column in which you report on local hiking areas.

In some cases, being an Average Joe or Jane is more of a selling point to editors. As a reader, I'd be more loyal to a columnist who experiences hiking as I would—a novice who loves to hike but is still learning—than an expert who considers novice hikes boring. If you want to introduce experts into your column, you might consider interviewing them on how to avoid mistakes commonly made by beginner hikers.

Whatever your credentials for being a columnist, remember to write and speak like an expert. Put away your self-doubts when you write. If you believe you are qualified to write a column, then do it with an authoritative voice.

13

8. *Effective columnists understand the bottom-line issues involved in publishing.* When proposing a column, consider how editors can use it to sell advertising. An editor may like your column, but that editor must sell it to her boss. With sound financial reasons under her belt, her chances of doing so increase.

   If you cover a subject that has products associated with it, use that information to sell your column. If you write about running, research how much is spent on advertising by running-gear manufacturers and present the information to the editor at the publication you're targeting. Such research could be the factor that pushes an editor to decide to publish your column.

9. *Effective columnists realize that editors must sometimes make changes to the copy.* Whether to make the copy fit a particular space or to conform with the style used by the publication, editors must occasionally alter the original copy. Due to time pressures, many columnists don't get to review their copy before it goes to press. That's not to say, however, that you shouldn't speak up if your column is being edited to the point where you no longer recognize it or it's no longer accurate.

10. *Effective columnists are persistent.* If an editor turns you down, but also gives you suggestions regarding your work, take the advice and continue. You'll be able to approach that publication again when you've revised your column to better suit the publication, or when the editor leaves for another opportunity—a common occurrence in the publishing world.

2 What Type of Column Do You Want to Write?

Have you been practicing a hobby for several years? Do you have a career that you love? Were you inspired to start a new career? Do you take vacations that make your friends say, "Wow, how do you dream up these trips?"

Hobbies are great sources for columns. They allow hobby enthusiasts to explore in detail the subtle nuances of their crafts. After eight years of studying karate, I took a good look at what I did, how I did it, how I would have liked to have done it better and decided to put it into book form. I could have just as easily written a column about my experiences in karate.

Careers are also terrific areas from which to draw material for a column. As the former editor of two business trade magazines, I can say without hesitation that it's tough finding business columnists who know a particular area well enough to write about it in an understandable, meaningful way. Say you own a janitorial service and want to write a column featuring health and safety tips in your industry—*Cleaning Business Magazine* may very well want to hear from you.

Experiences are yet additional areas to write about. If you have a knack for putting together low-cost excursions in and around your local area, the editor of your community newspaper may be interested. Or, try the editor of the monthly magazine covering your state.

If you draw inspiration from all three areas—hobby, career and experiences—consider pulling them together into a humor column or a commentary column. However, beware that the more general a column, the more difficult it is to sell.

A hobbyist column covering the latest accessories for train sets would be welcomed by a handful of publications, such as *Classic Toy Trains* magazine. On the other hand, a general humor column featuring the amusing highlights of your day-to-day life could run in lots of publications. The problem is it may not have enough of a slant to appeal to editors. Take that column and give it a specific focus, such as your experiences as a soccer coach for grade-school children, and it would be easier to place—in a free parenting publication, for instance.

That's not to say that being an expert in a specific area makes it easy to

---

Exercise

Assess your ability to cover a particular subject by generating ten column topics. For example, if I were to write a column targeted at women in the martial arts, my ten topics might look like the following:

1. The best martial arts styles for women.

2. Many women report an aversion to sparring. I'll tell readers how to spar safely and effectively.

3. Finding a school that takes women's concerns about the martial arts seriously.

4. An interview with the owner of the Karate School for Women, an all-women martial arts school in New York City.

5. What women lack in physical strength, they can make up for in stamina and speed.

6. Why strict rules on jewelry and hair clips are zealously enforced by martial arts teachers.

7. How to buy a well-fitting martial arts uniform.

8. Studying a martial art need not mean abandoning femininity—in fact, the martial arts can enhance it.

9. The results of a recent survey show why some women stick with their martial arts training and why others quit.

10. Why martial arts self-defense techniques are too choreographed to be of much use on the street.

I could go on and on. If I were proposing a column to the publisher of a monthly martial arts magazine, I'd already have a list of topics that don't overlap, compliment the subject niche I've chosen and can be expanded into full-length columns.

sell your column. You don't want to be a generalist, but you also don't want to be so specific that you limit your audience.

Say you're the editor of a monthly organic gardening magazine and you are approached by three writers proposing different columns for your publication.

The first columnist works at a nursery and is proposing a column based on her knowledge of the plants for which she cares. The second has studied the effects of compost on making plants grow and is proposing a column on that topic. The third columnist has turned her entire yard from a high-maintenance, chemical-dependent property consisting mostly of lawn, to one with no grass, but lots of trees, flowers and vegetable plants sustained naturally. She is proposing a column based on her experience, which she has recorded for the past five years.

The first proposal is too general. There's no angle, and chances are the magazine already covers the plants about which the writer plans to write. If the proposal had included rare or unique plant species, it might have a place in this publication.

The second proposal is too specific. It has an angle—the effects of compost on plants' growth. But it sounds more like a one-shot feature article than a monthly column.

The third proposal has the best potential. Unlike the first proposal, it has an angle, and it is not general. Unlike the second proposal, it is not so specific that it would be difficult to generate topics.

Types of Columns

It's not enough to know the subject you want to cover in your column. You have to know what columns are out there and what trends are affecting how your subject is being covered.

Following are twelve of some fifty categories of columns from the annual *Editor & Publisher's Directory of Syndicated Services*, which lists columns sold by syndicates. Included are the titles of columns being sold today, as well as trends within those categories that offer aspiring columnists ideas for developing their own columns.

1. Advice. The annual *Editor & Publisher's Directory of Syndicated Services* lists more than two hundred advice columns, ranging from *Ask Betty Crocker* to *Know Your Banker* to *Working Smarter*. With so

many advice columns out there, breaking into this cluttered category requires a good deal of ingenuity and imagination.

Working Wounded columnist Bob Rosner broke in by focusing on the workplace. By offering advice on coping with business colleagues, dead-end jobs, switching companies, performance pressures and being fired, Rosner tapped into the growing disgruntlement endemic in the workplace as a result of downsizings and mergers and acquisitions. (To learn how Rosner started in the column-writing business, read the interview on pages 104-107.)

2. Automotive. I've included this specific category because it has seen lots of growth in the past few years—and trends such as this offer the best opportunities for aspiring columnists.

   Automotive columns appeal to publishers because car advertisers represent a huge source of income. Some newspapers, *The New York Times*, for example, have begun publishing whole sections devoted to automobiles. The category is so popular that entire syndicates have emerged that specialize in car columns. No longer simply covering new products, these syndicates have turned specialization into an art.

   AutoWriters Associates Inc., Wilmington, Delaware, offers no fewer than ten columns on automobiles, covering new trucks and vans (*Truck Talk*); motor homes (*Rolling Homes*); classic vehicles (*Classic Classics*); maintenance (*Ask the Auto Doctor*); women's views (*Drive, She Said*); and add-on automotive products (*AfterMarket Reports*).

3. Business. Capitalizing on the trend toward self-employment and home-based businesses are such columns as *Promoting Your Business* and *Home Office Know-How*. What trends are around the corner? One trends forecaster predicts more corporations will become patrons of the arts in an effort to improve their images. A column on this might be welcomed by a local business publication.

   And though the columns listed here are sold mainly to newspapers, don't overlook trade publications when it comes to selling your business column. The "trades" represent a huge slice of the publishing pie. Focusing on occupations or industries, trade journals often pay fairly well. And trade editors may be more receptive to new columnists than editors of consumer publications, which include mainstream magazines and newspapers aimed at readers of general interest, sport, hobby and other specialized consumer interest material.

Read the trade journals covering your industry, and consider writing a column for one of them. You may have the support from your boss, who might be pleased to receive the free publicity. And if you're traveling with a laptop computer, you may find it a nice change of pace to write a column on the plane rather than reading the latest issue of *People* magazine.

If you're a consultant looking to attract clients via your column, you may find a home in a trade magazine related to your field of expertise. Be forewarned, however, that some editors steer clear of using consultants as columnists, because they feel that consultants are more interested in getting clients than with dispensing useful information. Why, then, is it common to see columns penned by consultants in so many trade magazines? Because consultants often write for free.

4. Family. The baby boom has spurred lots of interest among parents for information about child rearing and family-oriented editorials. Syndicated columns in this crowded category include *Children's Book Reviews, Parent to Parent, Taking the Kids, Daycare, Grandparenting, Families Today* and *Surviving Sane.*

    But there are lots of trends in this category that don't focus solely on children. Consider these: More couples are choosing cohabitation over marriage; the growing need for elder care; and the growth in shared housing in which habitants share cooking, child and elder care, gardening and even education responsibilities.

    You might write a column that shows readers how to apply shared-housing practices to their own communities. Such a column could discuss how to start a weekly community potluck supper arrangement, or a community garden, or how to negotiate reduced rates with a landscaping company to service all the homes on a particular block.

5. Computers. The computer category is popular among publishers because demand for computer-related information among readers is high and such columns generate advertising.

    Certainly, the explosion of the Internet has spawned lots of columns: *The Chat Room, What's Online* and *Webpointers* are just a few.

19

Some computer columnists have found success with niche columns: *Inside the Video Games*, *Computing for Kids* and *Surfing the Net With Kids*, which appeals to frightened parents whose children have access to the Web and all its adult-oriented material.

One growing area related to computers includes interactive, online learning in which people use their computers and specialized software to earn university degrees and to school their youngsters at home. Why not consider writing a column on this subject and how it is being used by some forward-thinking students? What makes these trends even more attractive to editors is their ties to another popular category: education.

6. Food and wine. Today, wine gets almost as much attention as the food we're supposed to eat with it. Among the wine columns syndicated today: *In Vino Veritas*, *Wine on the Table*, *Wine Scrapbook*, *Wine Talk* and *Wine Today*.

    Another popular area within this category is the fast-and-easy cooking columns. Examples include *Healthy 20-Minute Menus* and *Desperation Dinners*, which describe how to cook nutritious meals in less than half an hour.

    With so many different columns covering food and wine, how can you break in with a fresh angle? Start by looking at the trends toward "clean" food grown without chemicals; an increase in family "microfarms" that raise organic food; fast-food health-food restaurants; and Internet grocers that deliver food to shoppers' doorsteps.

7. Health, fitness and beauty. Syndicated columns in this category range from senior citizens (*Feel Young Again*, *Stay Alive Longer*), to disabilities (*Living With a Disability*), to family fitness (*The Fit Family*), to appearances (*Best Looks*), to more general fare (*The Health Insurance Troubleshooter*, *Understanding Your Health Insurance* and *The HealthCare Advocate*).

    This category is tough to break into simply because it is covered so thoroughly. But like computers and automobiles, this category attracts advertising dollars, and is therefore of interest to editors. Finding a unique angle is worth the effort.

8. Hobbies. Syndicated hobby-related columns range from sewing (*And Sew On*), to chess (*Chess Quiz*), to bridge (*Sheinwold's Bridge*), to stamps

and coins (*The Stamp and Coin Exchange*), to crafts (*Craft of the Week*), to collecting (*Kovels: Antiques and Collecting, The Collector*).

The widespread interest in hobbies has spawned many niche magazines devoted to specific hobbies. There's *American Woodworker*; *The Blade Magazine* for knife enthusiasts; *Classic Toy Trains*; *Crochet World*; *Dollhouse Miniatures*; *Knitting Digest*; *Linn's Stamp News*; *Plastic Canvas Crafts*; *Rug Hooking*; and *Teddy Bear Review*.

If you want to write about your hobby, familiarize yourself with the magazines that cover it. The editors of these magazines are always on the lookout for new material that presents a fresh viewpoint or angle.

9. House and home. As the home becomes more than just a place to hang your hat and transforms itself into the office, retreat and gym, more people are interested in improving it. That's why the "do-it-yourself" column has become so popular, with such offerings as *Home Improvement*, *This Old House*, and *Mr. Handyperson*.

    Another area within this category covers real estate. As with computers, real estate attracts advertising dollars and is thus attractive to publishers. Syndicated real-estate columns include *Mortgages* and *Your New Home*.

10. Humor. Humor may be subjective, and therefore, difficult to sell, but everyone needs a laugh, which is why humor columns remain popular. If you think you have a knack for writing humor columns, give it a try.

    To increase the chances of selling your humor column, make it specific. Publications have access to lots of general humor columns—from the famous, such as columns by Dave Barry and Russell Baker, to the less well-known, with such titles as *Grin 'n' Bear It* and *Don't Laugh, You're Next*. It may be easier to break in by writing specific humor columns, such as *Golf: Laughter on the Links*.

    What about writing a humor column about your career in sales and selling it to *Selling Power* magazine? The editor might jump at the chance to inject levity into the magazine. Of course, you might have to write it under a pseudonym, so your boss doesn't realize you're using his company as the target of your humor.

11. Religion. From *Ethics and Religion* to *Faith Matters* to *Saints and Sinners*, religious columns have flourished over the past few years.

21

If you're interested in this category, consider covering it from a fresh angle. The search for spiritual fulfillment has become a popular pursuit. One of the outcomes of this search has been a new mix-and-match approach to faith where believers borrow traits from different religions to create their own. A column profiling people who have adopted this approach to religion might be welcomed by an alternative newspaper.

12. Travel. The travel category illustrates just how specific columns have become. Consider the *The Business Traveler*, *Taking the Kids* and *RV Traveling*.

A return to the great outdoors has been a growing trend since the mid-'90s. A parenting paper might be interested in your column on family outdoor trips available in your local area.

Topics and Ideas to Grow On

As a columnist, you want to pique readers' interests without insulting them or going over their heads. At a National Society of Newspaper Columnists convention, *San Diego Union-Tribune* editor and writer Neil Morgan put it succinctly: "If a columnist doesn't get ahead of a community, there's little reason to come to work. If a columnist gets too far ahead, there's *no* reason to come to work."

The exercises below are designed to help you pique reader interest and expand your range of topics and ideas.

• *Develop the art of being as controversial as your audience will allow.* Some columnists have created a career around being controversial, but they are well aware of just how far they can go.

Exercise

Try writing a controversial column. You won't necessarily submit it to an editor, but it will give you a feel for whether you have a knack for handling this area of writing. Consider your audience and whether it would be put off by your writing or entertained by it.

If you'd rather not write a controversial column or feel your audience wouldn't tolerate it, try writing a column about a controversial topic. Approach it as a neutral observer and offer both sides of the controversy.

- *Inject variety into your work.* Just because you write one type of column—a how-to column, for example—doesn't mean you can't put a different spin on it once in awhile. If you write a hard-driving business column for salespeople seeking to increase their earnings, try writing a "softer" one chronicling your vacation and how rest and relaxation can contribute as much to success as hitting the pavement every day.

If you write a consumer-beware column that targets manufacturers of defective products, try writing one praising a particular company for honestly and proactively dealing with a problem with its product. If you write a column that consists of recipes that can be made in under fifteen minutes, try writing a recipe-free column that instead chronicles the history of how quick recipes came to be popular.

Exercise

Consider different types of columns: instructional/how-to, inspirational, humorous, advice, commentary, political/public affairs or current events and issues. Use one of these approaches in your work that you formerly haven't used.

- *An article is a column waiting to happen.* Good columnists can read any magazine and find column ideas in it. For example, if you write a column on gardening and read an issue of *Martha Stewart Living* magazine, you might decide to write a column with a humorous spin on it comparing your garden to Martha's. (Be careful, however, not to go overboard, writing about a person in a way that could be interpreted as slanderous.)

Exercise

Generate three column topics based on articles in a magazine unrelated to your column's subject.

- *Become a human version of your computer's word-search function.* Though related to the previous exercise, this one goes a step further, teaching you to train your eyes to locate words in an article that relate to the subject of your column. Indeed, there are lots of references to your subject hiding in publications unrelated to your area of expertise. By training your eyes to find them, you can increase your range of topics.

> ### Exercise
>
> Next time you're reading a magazine unrelated to your column's subject, skim the articles for words related to your area of expertise. For example, if you write a column on woodworking, train your eyes to find words related to that subject. You just might see a profile of a U.S. senator in the political magazine *George* that mentions his love of woodworking. Consider using an interview with the senator as a topic for your column.

- *Your columns—in book form.* The reason so many books are published consisting of previously published columns is because columns lend themselves well to book format. Look at the table of contents of three or four books, and note how each chapter lends itself to a column topic.

> ### Exercise
>
> A book publisher has just asked you to compile your favorite columns into a book. Write the table of contents. Each chapter should have the title of the column and a one- or two-sentence description. Make sure the topics flow smoothly and don't overlap or repeat themselves. This exercise forces you to incorporate variety and a logical continuity into your topics.

- *The title is half the job.* In addition to great writing, good columnists know how to write headlines that draw readers into their columns. Despite the fact that editors can, and often will, change your headlines, make a point of writing strong ones. Such a habit reinforces in an editor's mind that you're a conscientious, thoughtful writer. (See the Success Is in the Details section in chapter four for advice on writing headlines.)

> ### Exercise
>
> If you don't have headlines for your columns, write some. If you do, try improving them. Puns work well. A pun is nothing more than a play on words. For example, a column about art thieves who steal from tombs carried the headline "Raiders of the Lost Art"—a play on the title of the movie *Raiders of the Lost Ark*. Another column, about the move by environmentalists who see cattle grazing as preferable to development, carried this creative headline: "The New Eco Mooooovement."

- *There are no new ideas, only old ones with new angles.* When something is new, it tends to be written about extensively. The challenge becomes to write about a popular topic in a way no one else has.

Exercise

Find a fresh angle to a much-covered topic. For example, if you write a food column and don't want to write about organic food as everyone else is doing, consider writing about it from a different angle—perhaps that while organic food may be free of pesticides, it may, as a result, contain other contaminants, such as insects.

- *Be creative.* In addition to a print column, Dave Lieber, a columnist for the *Fort Worth Star-Telegram*, produces a video column that can be viewed via the Internet, as well as an audio column you can hear over the phone. It's innovations such as these that grab an editor's attention.

Exercise

Consider what you can do to make your column different from others in its category. If you aspire to write a column for a newspaper distributed in an area with a growing Hispanic or Asian community, consider penning a bilingual column. Though the newspaper may not be able to run it in its printed version due to space restrictions, it may carry it on its Web site.

- *Put a positive spin on a negative topic.* Though complaining may seem to be a national pastime, that doesn't have to carry over to your column. Indeed, it's easy to get caught up in criticism, particularly if you write a commentary or humor column.

But columnists shouldn't write negative pieces all the time. As Neil Morgan of the *San Diego Union-Tribune* said at the National Society of Newspaper Columnists convention: "Readers don't want to go along with you on a blood hunt every day. Not everyone is a villain. There are some good people out there, too."

Understanding the types of columns that are published is key to determining where your proposed column will fit. As you approach the point at which you will present your column proposal to an editor, it will help tremendously if you can exhibit your knowledge of the columns your work competes with and how your column differs from them. It's a small but important step in acquiring the kind of expertise editors expect from today's writers.

Exercise

Go over your list of topics for your columns, and count how many have a negative bent. If it's more than a third of your work, rethink your approach. How might you rework some of those columns to have a positive spin?

---

3 Get to Know the Markets

Understanding the kinds of publications published today is key to finding a home for your column. And "home" really does describe the kind of place you want for your column—a place where your hard work is appreciated by a loyal readership that eagerly anticipates your writing and where your editor looks forward to receiving your work. After all, you've undoubtedly spent countless hours compiling your columns, or you will if you haven't yet written them.

Perhaps the home for your column is a daily newspaper. Or maybe it's a community newspaper, or a trade magazine, or one of the growing "alternative" newspapers. The best place for your column may not be in print at all, but in an online magazine or newspaper. By taking the time to find the right publication for your column, you'll increase your chances of seeing it published and of attaining what you want—whether it's recognition, additional income, enjoyment or all three.

Daily Newspapers

Despite declining readership, most daily newspapers are doing well financially. The reasons are threefold:

• Many daily newspapers have established Web sites to promote themselves and to retain classified ad dollars that are being captured by various online services. According to the Newspaper Association of America, in 1998, more than eight hundred of the nearly sixteen hundred dailies in the United States had Web sites.

Newspaper Web sites offer aspiring columnists an "electronic" forum for their work. Since space is virtually unlimited on the Web, newspaper editors may be willing to run your columns on the paper's site. However, since few sites have yet to turn a profit, editors may not be willing to pay you to run your work there. However, the exposure from being published online may lead to other opportunities to get your work published.

Check out the Web site of your area's newspaper, or study the winners of the Newspaper Association of America's Digital Edge Awards, an annual competition that recognizes the achievements of the top online newspapers. For a listing of the winners, visit http://www.naa.org/feds/contests/index.html, and click "New Media Federation Digital Edge Awards." Then visit the papers' Web sites to see the kinds of subjects they cover and how they present them. (Please note that Web sites are subject to change. If the material cannot be located using the address provided, go to the home page of the site—usually found by using the address preceding the first slash—and try locating the information there.)

A warning about newspaper Web sites, or for that matter, any Web site operated by print publishing companies: If writers are published in print, the owners of those print products may feel entitled to use that material on their Web sites without compensating the writer. In 1996, Jack Eden pulled his *Garden of Eden* column from *The Washington Post* after ten years when he learned of the publisher's plans to run the column on its Web site without paying him an additional fee.

The case illustrates the tug-of-war print publishers and some freelance writers wage over "electronic rights." Some publishers feel that purchasing print rights automatically entitles them to electronic rights to the same editorial; some writers feel just the opposite.

• The second reason daily newspapers are faring well is because they have attracted readers by expanding coverage of popular topics. Take religion. After years of relegating religion to their back pages, America's daily papers have begun acknowledging the importance of faith in the lives of their readers. *The Charlotte Observer*, for example, hired a second religion writer to cover ethics and values and added a Saturday faith section that includes reviews of religion books, CDs and software.

Daily newspapers are also focusing more on local news. In a June 29, 1998, *New York Times* article, Gregory E. Favre, editor of *The Sacramento Bee*, said his paper spent more of its resources on local news than on anything else.

If you are trying to break into a daily newspaper, consider developing a column around local news. In his book, *The American Newspaper Columnist*, Sam G. Riley, professor of communication studies at Virginia Tech and a former columnist, writes: "Many papers in the 1990s badly need an injection of personality, or individuality. One of the means of filling this need is for the paper to employ a good local columnist." (Please see the Resources section for information on Riley's book.)

• Finally, daily newspapers are doing well because they have fought hard to keep young readers from deserting. Indeed, research shows that fewer teenagers and Generation Xers are reading newspapers than their counterparts did in the 1960s.

One way newspapers are attracting young readers is with a program called Newspapers in Education. The program exists at approximately half of all U.S. daily newspapers, including *The Tampa Tribune, Houston Chronicle, Chicago Tribune* and *The Seattle Times*, and consists of youth- and teen-oriented pages and sections. If the subject of your column is aimed at the young reader market, editors of daily newspapers may welcome your work.

Other papers are attracting young readers with technology columns and articles, some of which run on their Web sites. The *San Jose* (California) *Mercury News* operates "Digital High," a section of the newspaper's Web site created by "Silicon Valley Teens" (http://www.mercurycenter.com/digitalhigh/). It contains news, features, college information, opinion pieces and sports all written by teenagers. It even runs photos of its young free-lancers and an advertisement seeking more. If you're a young person who can write, chances are editors would be interested in what you have to say to your peers.

As for the pay scales at daily newspapers, a new, young local columnist would probably be paid on the low end. According to the *2000 Writer's Market*, daily newspapers pay $40 to $300 per column, with a mid-level range of $125 per column.

Community Newspapers

Like their daily counterparts, weekly community newspapers have experienced fairly steady growth, according to the National Newspaper Association, which found that the number of weekly papers rose slightly through the mid- to late '90s. This means weekly papers offer a reliable, steady market in which to make a name for yourself.

If you're willing to slant your column toward local news, but aren't sure of areas to cover, check out the Web site of the Suburban Newspapers of America (http://www.suburban-news.org/superlinks.html). You'll find a listing of members hyperlinked to their Web sites. Visit these papers, and study the topics they cover. Some of the topics I noted on a visit included home energy issues; local vacation retreats; profiles of active, locally based seniors; and local religion coverage.

"I'm always looking for people who can write about local issues," says Liz Parker, copublisher and executive editor of the Recorder Community Newspapers, Stirling, New Jersey, which consists of fifteen papers with a combined circulation of 60,000. Of the approximately twenty-five columnists who write for the papers, most are carried by more than one paper, says Parker.

Parker says she receives about fifty column solicitations per year and that perhaps 10 percent of them are useable. She says that three sample columns—none of which have to have been published—are enough to give her an idea if the work is suitable for her papers. "We don't require that our columnists be previously published," she adds.

Parker notes that it's difficult to find good writers. "It's gotten harder to find freelancers to cover night meetings, and it seems that everyone wants to be a humor columnist," she notes.

"Too often we get writers who want to be Erma Bombecks and write about a day in their lives. I'll run them, but I won't pay them," she says, referring to the fact that these kinds of columns are "interesting and well written," but so numerous that their creators will often give them away for free. When Parker does pay, she generally offers columnists thirty dollars to fifty dollars per column, each of which runs from 700 to 1,000 words— a good deal longer than columns that run in daily papers.

Still undecided whether to focus your talents on community papers? Consider what Parker says: "We've started a number of columnists who have gone on to larger papers, including *The New York Times*."

And don't underestimate the ability of community newspapers to keep up with their daily counterparts. Many operate their own Web sites, and publishers often own more than one paper. That means that in addition to being published in several community papers owned by one parent company, you may even find yourself being published on a community paper's Web site, thus extending your exposure well outside your community.

Alternative Weeklies

Alternative weekly newspapers, or "alts," are those often free, sometimes countercultural tabloids featuring thorough arts and entertainment coverage and investigative reporting. They range from the Atlanta-based *Creative Loafing* to New York City's *Village Voice* to Indiana's *Bloomington*

Voice and tend to have readers who are young, educated and active.

The alternative newspaper market is booming. According to the Association of Alternative Newsweeklies, the number of alternative newspapers is up, as well as circulation and ad revenues. That spells opportunity for aspiring columnists.

A case in point: *New York Press* started in 1988 with five full-time employees, publishing twenty-four pages a week. In 1998, it employed fifty-five people—ten of them on the editorial side and the rest in sales and management—publishing 120-page issues.

Interestingly, though some might assume that alts are purely left-of-center, some, like *New York Press*, run a varied, eclectic mix of editorial. For example, *New York Press* runs a column by a former *Village Voice* columnist with a pronounced Marxist viewpoint, as well as one by a writer from the conservative Washington, DC, magazine *The Weekly Standard*. The alt also runs a sex column; one featuring obscure historical facts; and one by its editor, who writes a column called *Mugger*, in which he denounces everyone from the president of the United States to magazine editors to waiters at expensive restaurants.

But just because a newspaper falls into the alternative category doesn't mean it's like all the other alts, according to a spokesman for the Association of Alternative Newsweeklies. "There are different papers with different needs, styles and approaches," he said.

"Some are more opinion; others heavy reporting," he continued. One thing they do have in common, however, is that they are all fairly local in coverage, he added, so there is little opportunity for someone to sell columns who doesn't live in the same city in which the paper is published.

Also, just because it's an alt paper doesn't mean it relies solely on freelance writers. *Phoenix New Times* hires full-time writers and reporters, so it might be more difficult to sell a column to that alt than to the *Chicago Reader*, which tends to rely on freelancers. The lesson: Know the publication to which you're targeting your column. Read it regularly, and note the bylines. Check to see if the bylined authors are staff writers or contributors by reading the paper's masthead, which lists members of the publication's staff and is usually located on the editorial page. If most are contributors, you can assume they are freelancers.

If you're interested in alternative weeklies, consider what Craig Hitchcock of the *Bloomington Voice* said in a May 31, 1997, *Editor & Publisher* article: "These papers often cover the stories that dailies don't or won't." If your column has been rejected by daily or community news-paper editors because it's too controversial, perhaps a better home for it lies with the alts.

Besides reading the alt in which you may be interested in being published, read trade magazines and the business press for articles on that particular publication. Publishing is not a static industry, and publishers are always seeking to redefine themselves. Take New York City's *Village Voice*, which spent more than twenty years building a national presence. Today, the *Voice* is abandoning its national circulation and is planning to stay local. This means the paper's editors will be looking for more locally based stories. Perhaps the editors will want more niche columns that cover areas the paper couldn't report on previously due to its national scope.

In addition to abandoning its national focus, the *Voice*, like many alts today, is contemplating expanding coverage into the suburbs—something many of these papers would have shunned in previous years. Consider the alts that already have a presence in the suburbs: *OC Weekly* (Orange County, California), *Eastsideweek* (Seattle) and the *Long Island Voice* (New York).

Like daily newspapers, alts are also consolidating. For example, Phoenix-based New Times Inc. owns seven papers: *New Times Los Angeles*, *SF Weekly* (San Francisco), *Dallas Observer*, *Houston Press*, *Miami New Times*, *Phoenix New Times* and *Westword* (Denver).

With large media companies buying up the alts, keep in mind that the papers' countercultural spin may be declining. To some people, alts are becoming more mainstream, so there may be a limit to how "creative" your columns can be. That said, read closely the alt you're interested in and note whether your work would fit with the rest of the editorial.

Giveaways

No longer your father's giveaway publication, today's giveaway papers are worth reading. I'm constantly amazed at the number of giveaway newspapers available in my area, covering everything from entertainment to New Age to family activities.

One of the hottest niches in giveaways is the so-called local "parenting" newspapers, which are typically published monthly and report on all aspects of community affairs related to family, including local school lunch programs, after-school activities, puppet shows and children's pool hours. Many are started as kitchen table projects by parents who want answers to their own questions about children.

These publications have quickly moved from the kitchen table to the portfolios of large media firms. During 1997 alone, eleven parenting papers were sold, mostly to established media companies, according to the Parenting Publications of America, a trade association representing regional parenting publications.

What's more, some of these media companies own more than one of these types of papers. For columnists, this means that should you get your foot in the door of one of these papers, you could be published in several of them. Starting in a growing niche is a great way to build your reputation quickly, and it may even offer an "in" into a full-time writing position—if that's what you're seeking.

Additional Newspapers

Newspapers are not limited to dailies, community papers, alts and giveaways. Some newspapers specialize in business, religion, government and college life. To get an idea of the variety of newspapers available, visit Newspapers Online! at http://www.newspapers.com.

Newspapers Online! lists everything from major daily newspapers to trade journals to business publications to college and university newspapers to religious publications. Under "specialty publications," I found thirty-two newspapers, ranging from *Linn's Stamp News* for stamp hobbyists to the *The Riverview Times* for people who want "news of the Upper Mississippi River."

Magazines

With more than eighteen thousand consumer and business magazines being published in the United States, this outlet would seem to offer aspiring columnists plenty of opportunities. However, those opportunities are limited to columnists who can grasp the tightly focused niche that most magazines cover and who can fine-tune their columns to address that niche market.

Consumer Magazines

Consumer magazines are aimed at readers of general interest, sport, hobby or other specialized consumer interest material, as opposed to magazines aimed at business, professional and trade interests. Consumer magazines cover everything from animals (*Dog Fancy, Horse Illustrated, Pets—Part of the Family*) to fitness (*Healthstyle, Men's Health*) to travel (*Historic Traveler, International Living, Islands*).

Breaking into consumer magazines is tough. The editors of these publications have established a strong, faithful readership and are unlikely to give an unknown writer editorial space in every issue. It's often best to start with a feature article or a column that is not written by a regular columnist. Check *Writer's Market* to find out which columns are open to freelancers. It's worth the effort, since breaking into a consumer magazine would ensure you a decent rate of pay and tremendous exposure.

If the topic of your column is specific—say your column is about knitting—it may best fit in a niche magazine. Indeed, the magazine world is filled with niche publications aimed at small groups of readers. Examples include *Cottage Life* for people who spend time at waterfront cottages throughout Canada and bordering U.S. states; *California Game & Fish*; *Today's Catholic Teacher*; and *Bluegrass Unlimited*, which covers bluegrass and old-time country music.

But just because the subject of your column is specific, don't rule out magazines not specifically geared toward that subject. For instance, if you write about travel to historic sites, don't rule out nontravel-related magazines. *Early American Homes* seeks pieces such as those and might welcome your column on a regular basis.

In addition to listing consumer magazines, *Writer's Market* lists the names of many niche magazines, along with information on submitting features and columns. Using this reference book, you can find out what the editors of niche magazines are looking for and whether they accept article and/or column submissions.

Trade Magazines

Trade magazines are published for people in a certain business or profession and are also known as business, technical and professional journals. They cover everything from advertising and public relations to collectibles to truck driving. Since they represent a field with less competition than consumer magazines, they offer good potential for columnists. Some even offer payment that rivals those of well-known consumer magazines.

A trade journal may represent an entire industry, such as printing, or it may be aimed at people in the same job who may or may not be employed in the same industry, such as salespeople. Trade journals can be company publications read by employees and/or stockholders, association publications read by members of an association, or they can be independently published.

If you're in a particular business, familiarize yourself with the publications covering your industry. Trade publications provide a particularly good area to break into as a columnist, but you need a solid grasp of the field it covers. Readers of trade journals are well-versed in their fields and will catch you if you make a mistake.

People who know an aspect of a particular field well enough to write a column on it are a rare breed. The ultimate "find" for a trade journal editor is acquiring someone who has a specialty—for example, human resources as it relates to companies with twenty-five or fewer employees—and can write about it in a way that interests and informs readers. If you have such a specialty, consider writing about it in your column.

Online Publications

Not long ago, online publications were simply reproductions of their print counterparts. They offered their readers glimpses of some of the articles in current print issues, access to articles from previous print issues or the opportunity to E-mail staffers of a particular publication. Today, you can find print publications' companion online magazines that feature high percentages of original writing.

Some large publishers publish online versions of their magazines under an original online brand. For example, magazine publisher giant Conde Nast publishes the online versions of its magazines *Gourmet* and *Bon Appetit* under the online brand Epicurious Food, http://www.epicurious.com, with 80 percent original content. If the editor of a print publication rejects your column, check if the editor of the online version will run it.

In addition to online versions of print publications, thousands of online publications have no print counterpart. They range from the well-known magazine *Slate* with twenty thousand subscribers to less well-known publications with several hundred subscribers.

Because online publications are still a relatively new phenomenon, the editors of these periodicals may be willing to take greater risks with columnists than print editors. But be aware that few publishers are making a profit from being on the Web. That means they may be less inclined to offer a decent rate for your work—or any pay at all. However, if you're willing to use this forum to get a foothold into column publishing, it may pay off as these ventures begin to generate profit for their owners.

Keep in mind that the online format enables columnists to involve themselves with their readers in ways that print columnists cannot. If you land a

35

slot on an online publication, your editor may expect you to possess a high level of Web sophistication. The editor may ask you to participate in real-time chats with your readers, involve someone you have interviewed for your column in a live chat with readers, field questions on a bulletin board, incorporate audio and video into your column or include hyperlinks in your column. (A hyperlink is a word or image that can be clicked on to send Internet users to another page or site.)

If you have access to the Internet and are open to writing a column for an online magazine, check out these resources:

• John Labovitz's E-Zine List contains more than twenty-three hundred online magazines searchable by title, subject or keywords. You can even hyperlink directly to a particular publication by clicking the title. (http://www.meer.net/~johnl/e-zine-list/index.html)

• The Etext Archives is home to electronic texts of all kinds, from the "sacred to the profane, from the political to the personal," according to its site. Click on "E-Zines" to gain access to thousands of electronic periodicals. (http://www.etext.org)

• AJR NewsLink is operated by the American Journalism Review and offers hyperlinks to more than fifty online magazines. (http://ajr.newslink.org)

Newsletters

According to the Newsletter Publishers Association, there are five thousand to eight thousand subscription newsletters in the United States and Canada. If you include nonsubscription newsletters, that number jumps to twenty-five thousand newsletters.

By their nature, newsletters tend to be short. Therefore, they do not have the luxury of lots of space to publish material. In many cases, it may be easier to get a short article published in a newsletter, then use that to sell yourself as a columnist to another type of publication.

Also, since most newsletter publishers get their revenues from subscriptions—and an annual subscription can run into hundreds of dollars—they are less likely to give their limited space to a new voice than, say, a weekly newspaper that derives its revenues from advertising and is distributed free to homes in a particular area.

However, some newsletters do run items from readers. This may be one way to get in if you have your heart set on a particular newsletter. After you have several items published, you may want to approach the publisher about writing a column.

Or you could take the route of some columnists and start your own newsletter. Travel writers Gene and Adele Malott publish *The Mature Traveler* newsletter, then use material from that publication for their column of the same name, which is syndicated by The New York Times Syndication Sales Corporation.

Michael Webb launched the *RoMANtic Newsletter* in 1996, offering advice for the "romance-impaired." He cultivated a list of about ten thousand subscribers before self-syndicating the *RoMANtic Column* two years later. (In self-syndication, a columnist sells her own work to newspapers and magazines; syndication involves a company that handles the work for the columnist. Both aspects are detailed in chapter nine.)

Understanding the types of publications produced today is an essential step toward finding a home for your column. Taking the time to evaluate these markets is a worthwhile step that will move you that much closer to seeing your column in print or in an online form.

4 Research Before You Write

Imagine the utter horror at having written six sample columns, then discovering someone else writes a column similar to yours for the publication you've targeted as ideal for your column. Or imagine accepting an offer by your local paper to run your column for free when a niche magazine would have paid you for the privilege. Rather than let fates such as these befall you, do a little research before submitting your column to a publication.

Find a Home for Your Work

Conducting research prior to submitting your column to a publication will dramatically increase your chances of finding the ideal home for your work while ensuring that you receive top dollar. It will also ensure that you follow the best path to your goal—whether it's to see one of your columns published, become a regular columnist for a particular publication, write for a newspaper syndicate, see your columns published in book form or land a full-time writing job that allows you to write about what you love.

If your goal is to write a column for a specific magazine, subscribe to it. When it arrives at your home, read it, then read it again. Study the writing. Is it breezy or businesslike? Do the topics overlap with yours? Would your column lend a unique new angle to the publication?

Study the masthead, usually found at the beginning of magazines or by the editorial page in newspapers. Check if there is an editor who specializes in the subject of your column. If there is, direct your queries to that editor. (Chapter eight details how to approach an editor with your work.)

Go to your library, and read back issues to see how the publication has changed. If the magazine has undergone a recent revamping, consider how the subject of your column fits with the new format. If the publication has changed its focus or slant—something all successful publications occasionally do—and no longer complements your column, revise it to fit the new publication, or target another publication.

Look up the publication in *Writer's Market*, and note whether its editors accept columns written by freelancers. Getting published in the magazine once—even if it's not in the capacity in which you want—will establish you as a capable writer who knows her subject and will introduce you to an editor at the publication to whom you may eventually pitch your column idea.

Exercise

A great way to prove to an editor that you know your subject is by writing an article related to it.

Writing an article and getting it published says a lot about your commitment to writing a column. If you have the wherewithal to flesh out a topic for an article, sell the idea to an editor, write it, then submit it for publication, you clearly have most of what it takes to write a column. (The list on pages 11-14 notes the qualities required of effective columnists.)

Such an exercise also helps establish early on whether your proposed topic is applicable to the column format. If, after writing the article, you find that you've said just about all you can on the subject, you've discovered that your column idea wasn't a column at all, but an article.

Casting Your Net

If you're not sure where to place your column, look at the nature of it, which will often indicate where it could run. If it's general, meaning it would appeal to a wide audience, cast your net wide. For example, if your column consists of social commentary, you might be better off starting with a publication that reaches a wide readership, such as a regional, local or giveaway newspaper. If you have no luck placing your column, you might need to refine its subject.

If the subject of your column is specific, meaning it would appeal to a narrow audience, you won't have to cast your net as wide. You will, however, want to spend lots of time researching the publications that may welcome your work, since there may only be a handful of them. You might look into association and trade publications, niche magazines and perhaps newsletters—all of which thrive on covering narrow subjects in detail.

Find out if someone is writing a column similar to the one you're proposing. Your local library should have a copy of *Editor & Publisher's Directory of Syndicated Services*, which will tell you if someone writes a syndicated column similar to yours. If your library doesn't have a copy, you can purchase one directly from *Editor & Publisher*. New editions are published in August. (See the Resources section for ordering information.)

As I noted in chapter two, *Editor & Publisher's Directory of Syndicated Services* lists syndicated columns and their authors. You can look up columnists by their names, by category and by the title of the column. Look under the category that relates to yours, and scan through the columns. If one of the columns sounds similar to yours, call the syndicate that handles the columnist and inquire about the column. (In some cases, the "syndicate" might consist of just the columnist.) Ask: "What is the thrust of the column? Where does it run? Can I get some sample copies?" If they won't provide you with samples, get a copy of the paper on the day when the column runs. If the paper has a Web site, it might make the columns available there.

If you see a column that complements yours, find out the name of the company that syndicates it, and consider submitting your column to that syndicate. Some syndicates specialize in particular areas, and you may find comfort in working for a syndicate that employs writers with a passion for the subject you write about. For example, Creative Syndication Services, Eureka, Missouri, specializes in columnists who write about hobbies, and Auto Page Syndicate, Emmaus, Pennsylvania, focuses on columns related to automobiles.

Cover All Your Bases

If I were interested in writing a column about women in the martial arts, I would look under "sports" and "women's pages" in the directory. I would discover that there are no other columns being syndicated that resemble my proposed column. This tells me that there is probably no demand for such a column in the syndicate market, because the topic of my column is too specific for general newspapers. I would be better off checking the magazine market.

To do that, I would check out the *Gale Directory of Publications and Broadcast Media*, which contains listings of newspapers and magazines in the U.S., their circulations and the names of departmental editors. It also includes listings of major syndicates with address and phone numbers.

To expand my search, I would refer to the *Standard Periodical Directory*. It classifies by subject eighty-five thousand U.S. and Canadian periodicals, including magazines, journals, newsletters and association publications. Both of these reference works are expensive and are often available in public libraries.

For more specific information on the association market, check out the *Encyclopedia of Associations: National Organizations of the U.S.*, which contains 135,000 listings covering everything from your local chamber of commerce to the Academic Institute of Rome. You can locate associations in this reference work by looking under the subject category that describes your work. Under each association is a listing of the periodicals it publishes.

If you'd like an affordable reference book that you can keep on your home bookshelf, consider purchasing *Writer's Market*. Many of the listed publications describe opportunities for freelancers to contribute columns to the publication. Even if the publication uses different writers for the same column, it is a chance for you to break in and get published and to possibly contribute enough columns so that the editor makes you the sole writer of the column or gives you your own column.

Another useful directory is the *Free Paper Publisher/Community Publications Yearbook*, an annual directory listing U.S. and Canadian weekly, community, free, niche and alt publications. As I mentioned in chapter three, many of these publications are thriving, attracting the highly desirable young reader audience, and often take chances the larger newspapers and established magazines won't.

If you haven't ruled out newsletters, check out the *Oxbridge Directory of Newsletters*, which lists 25,000 newsletters in the U.S. and Canada by subject area, or *Newsletters in Print*, which contains descriptions of more than 11,500 newsletters in the U.S. and Canada.

If you're targeting newspapers, consider subscribing to *Editor & Publisher* magazine, which covers the newspaper industry, including newspaper syndicates. It will keep you apprised of the latest columns being bought and sold. Or make it a habit to browse through the latest copies at your library.

Writer's Digest magazine is a must-read for aspiring columnists. It alerts freelancers to new publications, offers sound writing advice and discusses the business side of writing. (For more information on this and other publications mentioned here, see the Resources section.)

Success Is in the Details

As an editor at The New York Times Syndication Sales Corporation, I edited hundreds of columns—all of which ended up in a variety of newspapers and magazines around the world. Since so many different publications ran the columns, I did not have to concern myself with editing the copy to fit a particular slot in a particular publication. Therefore, I edited for style, clarity, content and other basics.

When I became an editor for an association magazine, my editorial responsibilities grew. Now I had to edit columns to fit a particular space. That meant deleting or adding copy, writing headlines, ensuring that the tone of the copy fit the tone of the entire publication, making sure that bulleted items didn't fall awkwardly in the copy and inserting editorial devices called "subheads" and "callouts" (see pages 44-45).

Most columnists whose material I edited did not take any of these details into consideration. They would turn in columns that met my word-count requirements, but their headlines were, for the most part, useless—they were too long, too short, too vague or just plain dull.

It's safe to assume that most editors consider it part of their job to write headlines that fit and to see to all the other small, but time-consuming details that go into preparing a column for publication. However, you can do yourself a great service and give yourself a leg up on the competition by paying attention to these details.

If you target a particular publication as ideal for your column, taking the time to work your column to fit the publication may go a long way toward getting your column published. Assuming that the writing is good and complements the publication, editors will be more inclined to run your column if they don't have to spend a lot of time preparing it for publication.

That said, let's go through the editorial details discussed. If you've targeted a certain publication for your column, get hold of three or four of the latest copies, and examine them for the following:

Word Count

When I was an editor at The New York Times Syndication Sales Corporation, the length of a column was 750 to 850 words. That was in the 1980s. In the 1970s, it wasn't unusual for a column to run 1,000 words. Today, most columns listed in the *Editor & Publisher's Directory of Syndicated Services* are 650 to 700 words, and many are no more than 500 words.

There are several reasons for the decline in word count. Some papers reduced the size of their pages to save on the cost of paper, while others redesigned their pages, and in doing so decreased the amount of space available for columns. Shorter columns give editors more flexibility to use pull quotes and art. In addition, shorter columns enable publishers to devote more space to advertising. Finally, shorter columns appeal to readers' shorter attention spans.

It's important to know the word count of the columns that run in the publication you have targeted. If need be, physically count the words. To save time, count the number of words in ten lines and divide by ten. Then, multiply that number by the number of lines in the column.

Word counts are estimates, and as such, you rarely, if ever, can expect your words to fit exactly into a particular space—unless the publication running your column can stretch or decrease the space as needed. Newspapers may be able to do this more easily than a magazine, whose page formats are more set.

If the word count on columns of the publication you've targeted is 650 to 700 words, and your columns are approximately 700 words long, consider noting for the editor which paragraphs can be cut if the column runs too long. This is an especially good idea for columnists who write commentary or humor pieces, where it's not as obvious where to cut versus recipe columns, where an editor would know to cut from the introductory or concluding copy, leaving the recipe untouched.

If you have already written several sample columns, do a word count on them. If the word counts differ greatly—say they range from 500 to 900 words—bring them in line with the word count for the publication you've targeted. If your columns are stored on your computer, save the original version in case your targeted publication rejects your columns, and your second choice runs columns that are longer than the first targeted publication.

If you find it difficult to beef up the shorter columns, consider scrapping them. If you can't bring yourself to cut the longer columns, you may be in for a long, hard journey. There are few columnists whose work isn't subject to the cutting board. Sure, it takes longer to write shorter, but it's a skill every columnist must perfect.

Headlines

Headline writing is an art. There are writers whose sole job is to write headlines. Effective headlines draw readers into a column and make them want to read the copy.

For example, consider a legal column that ran in a trade magazine on the use of surveillance cameras in the workplace. The writer submitted the column with the headline "Surveillance Cameras Monitor Workers"; it was changed to "Smile, and Say, 'Where Is the Hidden Camera?'" The latter headline serves to infuse a fresh perspective into the column, which, in this case, is written by a labor attorney. With legal matters generally being dry topics, injecting levity lightens up an otherwise dull topic and draws in readers who might otherwise not want to learn about the latest legal ramifications of using surveillance cameras in their workplaces.

Another word on headlines: Make sure they are not redundant. If you're writing for *Organic Gardening* magazine, don't mention the words "organic" or "gardening" in your headline. It's a given that the editorial inside the magazine will cover these subjects. Instead, focus on words that differ from those commonly found in the magazine. Such a headline-writing technique draws readers into the copy.

Finally, no matter how many hours you've spent perfecting your headline, your editor may change it. Whether it didn't "click" with the editor or space restrictions meant having to cut it, you may not see your headline in print. Still, taking the time to write a strong headline is worthwhile because it positions you as a conscientious, professional writer—the kind of person editors are more likely to want to work with.

Subheads

When pertaining to periodicals, subheads refer to the brief explanatory headlines, usually one line long, that appear periodically in the main body of a column or an article. A subhead breaks up the body copy. Like headlines, subheads are designed to draw readers into the copy. They are also used to stretch out a column that is running short.

Subheads generally appear before paragraphs that start a new thought or idea. The subheads in this book offer a perfect example of how they make the copy more readable. Note that they are no longer than five or six words—although they are often shorter in magazines and newspapers due to tighter space restrictions.

Avoid using words in the subhead that appear in the headline. The subhead is different from the headline. It alerts readers as to what is coming up next, and therefore, shouldn't echo what has already been stated in the headline.

Since subheads often run in type that's larger than the type found in the body copy, count the amount of characters that would fit in a subhead in the publication you've targeted. Then write your subheads to fit.

One way to develop good subhead-writing skills is to pay attention to the subheads in the periodicals you read. Note how often they appear in a column and how they work with each other. For example, in a column chronicling the daily events of a fly fisherman, the subheads consisted of a date and time. After a brief introduction, the column featured the subhead *June 12, 5:45 A.M.* and continued using this format until the column ended with the subhead *June 17, 3:15 P.M.*

Callouts

Callouts are snippets of text lifted from the body copy of the column and often placed in the middle of the page on which the column appears. They give readers more insight into the topic of the column and draw them into reading it. A reader will often read the headline first, then be drawn to the callout. Therefore, the callout is another device to draw in the reader, especially if the headline doesn't do the trick.

Quotes make for effective callouts. If you interviewed someone for your column and that person said something controversial or provocative, consider noting this for the editor. However, don't use a quote out of context simply to draw readers to the column. When they realize you've tricked them into reading the column, they may never return.

As with headlines and subheads, check your targeted publication to see how it uses callouts.

Sidebars

A sidebar consists of copy that's shorter in length than the column or article it accompanies. It may elaborate on the human interest aspects of the story, explain one important facet of the story in more depth or provide additional factual information—such as a list of names and addresses—that would read awkwardly in the body of the column. For example, if you write a column on collecting folk art, you might include a sidebar on books pertaining to that topic or the history of a particular piece of art from its beginning as a toy to part of a display in a museum.

Graphically, a sidebar is often boxed, bordered or set in a different typeface from the main copy and is usually given a title separate from that of the main column. If you include a sidebar in your column, remember to count the text as part of your total word count.

More Than Meets the Eye

Studying how a publication uses headlines, subheads, callouts and sidebars makes one realize how much additional work goes into a column other than writing the body copy. Consider a column in the monthly business magazine *Fast Company* that offers moving tips for workers who have been relocated. The headline, *Move It, Soldier!*, hints at the subject of the column without giving it away completely. This piques readers' interests enough to make them want to read on.

Though there is no callout, a second headline *(Common Sense From Uncle Sam)* beneath the main headline is more specific. Neither the first nor the second headline spell out exactly what the column is about. Rather, they entice readers to continue reading to find out the subject of the column, which, in this case, is advice from the U.S. military on how to move fast when an army base closes.

Subheads segment the tips into time frames. Readers learn the steps the U.S. military takes "Before the Move," "During the Move" and "After the Move." A sidebar, "Movers and Shakers," profiles a relocated employee's house-hunting experience. Taken together, the main headline, second headline, subheads and sidebar strengthen the body copy of the column.

Bios

If the publication you've targeted tags at the end of its columns a "bio"— short for biography—on the columnist, then write one for yourself that matches the format and positions you as an expert. Avoid accomplishments that don't relate to your area of expertise.

If you're writing a column on fly-fishing, don't mention that you are employed as an accountant. You could mention the number of years you've fly-fished, and if space allowed, additional information such as awards you've won pertaining to your sport.

If the publication runs photos of its columnists, consider having a photo of yourself taken that matches the ones found in the targeted publication. Many publications today tend to run informal photos of writers, so you may be able to save yourself the expense of a professional photographer. If you don't want to include a photo with your column, consider inserting this tag line at the end of your columns: "Photo of columnist available upon request."

❦

If you go to the trouble to note these small, but important, editorial details, by all means note so in your "pitch" letter, which I'll describe in chapter eight.

Editors will appreciate this attention to detail, and it may be the extra nudge they need to decide to give you a try. Certainly, if I was an editor who liked the subject and writing style of an aspiring columnist's work, knowing the writer cared enough to format his work to match that of other writing in my publication would spur me to recommend running his column.

PART TWO

Writing the Column

5 Getting Ideas

In the first part of this book, you learned about the kinds of columns that are written, the markets available for columns, how to locate the publications that would best serve your work and how to format your column to appeal to editors.

Now it's time to start writing.

For some, writing is the toughest part. Conducting the research and marketing their work is a breeze for these individuals, compared to sitting in front of their computer screens, waiting for the words to flow from their minds to the keys. This section is designed for those writers. But it's also designed for all types of writers because it will help you engage your audiences, strengthen the structure of your columns and generate ideas.

Certainly, columns are only as strong as their writers' ideas—and columnists need a lot of ideas, especially if they write a weekly column. Learning where to look for new ideas, how to look for them and how to record them are important steps in the column-writing process. When you get to a point where you are constantly generating and sorting through new ideas, you're less likely to suffer from writer's block or burnout.

Where Do Ideas Come From?

How you generate ideas depends on the type of column you write. If it is based on a particular industry, you would rely on press releases, industry contacts, trade periodicals and related seminars and conferences. If the column covers the social activities in your community, you would find new ideas by attending charity balls, dedications and other area events, as well as developing contacts with key people in your community.

Dona's Kitchen Kapers columnist Dona Z. Meilach generates ideas by "reading, being aware of what's going on, press releases, listening to people's needs and traveling." Adele Malott, who with her husband, Gene Malott, writes *The Mature Traveler*, says the travel industry generates the ideas for their columns. "It is news-based," she notes. (For the complete interview with the Malotts, please see pages 112-113.)

As a columnist, my problem is not generating ideas, but recording them. Ideas enter and exit my head so quickly that if I don't jot them down immediately, they're as good as gone. In fact, I seem to generate ideas everywhere but in my office, where it's most convenient to record them. I've corrected the situation by scattering pens and forty-nine-cent notepads throughout my house. I also keep pen and paper in my car and knapsack and have been known to take paper and pen with me when I run or walk, since any form of exercise triggers my creativity. When I can't locate a piece of paper, I'll jot down an idea on the palm of my hand.

Your Responsibility

Why make the process of generating ideas so all-consuming? Because no one else will do it for you.

When I was an editor for an association trade magazine, I would sit around a conference table with other editors every quarter and spend entire mornings or afternoons planning an issue. We would bring folders containing article clips, scribbled notes and other research chronicling topical issues and current trends we believed would be of interest to our readers. We'd discuss the topics we felt the magazine's columnists should cover, sometimes creating a list of two or three topics for each columnist to choose from.

Later, an editor would present those ideas to the columnists. Sometimes the columnists would accept one of our ideas, and other times they would ignore them.

Then we got smart.

We asked ourselves, Why should we do all the legwork for our columnists when they're the ones who know their subjects better than we do? In other words, why should we do their jobs? So instead of trying to be the experts, we let the experts be the experts. Now, instead of calling the magazine's tax columnist and asking if he would consider any of my ideas, I would say: "We're planning the next issue of the magazine and need copy two weeks from today. What do you want to write about?" Rarely didn't he have ideas. And if he had none, he would ask for time to think it over and call me back with a topic.

That worked nicely for a long time—until I was asked to assume responsibility for writing the magazine's environmental column. Now I could no longer pick up the phone and ask a columnist to generate a topic and write 800 words on it. I was the one who was expected to generate a topic and write the column.

Over the two years I wrote the column, which was titled *Environmental Concerns*, I learned how to generate ideas and cultivate sources—two skills that are critical to a columnist's success. Indeed, generating ideas is easy compared to fleshing them out using verifiable, reliable sources.

Go to the Source

Sources are people or things from which an author obtains information. When used in a column, sources provide evidence that the information is reliable. However, just because someone is quoted in a column doesn't mean that what he said is true or accurate. By identifying the person, the columnist allows readers to decide for themselves whether the information the source provides is reliable.

If you write a column on quilting, for example, you may find yourself seeking advice from someone more knowledgeable than yourself about a particular type of quilt. Having a list of sources you've acquired and kept current will help you enormously. By including quotes from these knowledgeable sources, you will become known among your readers as an expert at finding answers to difficult questions.

Sources don't have to hold advanced degrees or lofty positions. A source could be your next-door neighbor if you're writing a social commentary column about life in the suburbs. However, avoid using sources who aren't relevant to your column—the Ph.D. you quoted simply because he's a friend of yours or because you thought the title would impress readers.

Sources can even be readers. *Working Wounded* columnist Bob Rosner, who says he receives about one hundred reader letters a day, notes that they frequently provide him with ideas. But that wasn't always the case. "When you don't have people writing you letters, you use [as sources] your friends, contacts and people you meet on bus rides. That's what I did when I started doing this," he says.

When I assumed responsibility for writing *Environmental Concerns*, my most reliable sources were people in my industry who worked in the environmental field. I met them at industry conferences, both on the floor where environmental companies were displaying their latest wares and in conference seminars. I also cultivated government sources whom I'd meet at meetings held in Washington, DC.

In most cases, my sources were more knowledgeable and established than myself, which raises another point: Columnists cannot be intimidated by their sources. Those who are will find themselves detached from the very subject they profess to cover so well. Whether it's an official from the U.S. Environmental Protection Agency, the president of a company or a renowned professor from a prestigious university, as a columnist you cannot be afraid to approach them.

Some of the best material I acquired for my column came from informal conversations with top industry sources I met at a meeting or managed to get through to over the phone. In fact, I've often been surprised by how easy it was to not only get hold of CEOs on the phone, but how helpful and forthcoming they have been. Don't hesitate to pick up the phone and try to reach the top person in the industry you cover. Just be sure you know what to ask, and ask it quickly and professionally.

While quotes from CEOs and federal officials can lend an air of importance to your column, they can also make the column sound overly formal. To "humanize" a column, try using an anecdote, which is nothing more than a short narrative revealing a curious, amusing or insightful incident that illustrates the point of the column.

Following is an example of a *Working Wounded* column by Bob Rosner that opens with an anecdote that advises how to criticize someone at work:

> Timothy Lobdell taught me the key to offering criticism at work. Timothy isn't a therapist or a consultant. He's a convict who made headlines recently for his failed attempt to escape from a Fairbanks, Alaska jail. Oh, Timothy got out of the jail all right. But according to the "News of the Weird," it was the expletive tattooed on his cheek in inch-high letters that made him a cinch to recapture.
>
> Well, just like Timothy, most of us come to work with things tattooed all over our faces. Our biases, blind spots and BS can often be seen a mile away by the people we work with. That's why it's always a good idea to look in the mirror before offering criticism to others.

I relied heavily on anecdotes for my environmental column. They added interest to the sometimes dull information that had to be included in a column. Surely, describing how an eye-wash station saved the eyesight of a printing press operator who accidentally sprayed a chemical into his eyes adds interest to a column covering the topic of federal eye safety regulations.

Not all aspiring columnists can afford the time or money it takes to attend conferences, seminars and meetings. The following places and resources will help you find sources and generate ideas:

Libraries

Few people have time to spend hours browsing through shelves of library offerings. That's why when you go there, you want to have a plan. If you can spare only twenty minutes, don't wander over to the classical CDs when you came to research your column on bird-watching (unless, that is, you plan to incorporate the topic of classical music into your column).

If I was gathering ideas for my environmental column, I would scan the titles of the latest books, which are shelved in one area. If there were any environmental-related books, I'd check out the table of contents, looking for keywords that relate to the subject of the column, such as "business," "industry" and "companies."

Then I would go to the magazine section, selecting the latest issues of environmental and business magazines (after all, my column covers environmental regulations for businesses). The nice thing here is that, unlike a bookstore or newsstand, you can glance at past issues. Why would you want to look through past issues of magazines? For background information. Maybe you want to write a column on how a particular field has changed over the years. Past issues would provide you with some of the information you needed.

If I had time, I'd check newspaper business sections. Ideally, you want to read the entire contents of each paper, but realistically, you probably can't. However, keep in mind that lots of ideas can be generated by looking in obscure places. Even the classified ads can be sources of ideas. In my case, I might notice an unusually high number of job openings for environmental managers. The topic of my column could examine whether more printing companies are seeking such employees and, if they are, how to find them.

Finally, I'd log on to the library's computer system. Libraries have become incredibly savvy when it comes to technology. My local library is electronically connected to all the public libraries in my area. I can search for, and reserve, books from almost one hundred libraries, which will send my selections to my local library where I can pick them up.

Same goes for magazines. I can search through hundreds of magazines using keywords that describe the subject of my column. I can access full-length articles on CD-ROMs, then print them out. If you're not up to speed on this technology, ask a librarian to show you.

Bookstores

Bookstores are like the new-books section of your local library, except larger. Not only do bookstores allow you to research the latest information on the subject you cover in your column, but they've become literary community centers where you can have a cup of coffee and hear your favorite author speak. If your bookstore features guest authors who cover the same subject as you, attend those events and try to meet the author. Maybe you can get an interview with him, either there on the spot or over the phone at a time convenient to both of you.

Trade Publications

Often not carried by local libraries and newsstands, trade publications are published for people in a certain business or profession. As such, they tend to cover a subject in the kind of detail a consumer publication never would. Two trade publications I subscribe to are *Editor & Publisher*, which covers the newspaper industry, and *Publishers Weekly*, which covers the book publishing industry. Both are available at my local library, although most trade publications are not carried by libraries because too few patrons would be interested in them.

They're also expensive. An annual subscription can easily run over one hundred dollars. If you can't afford a subscription to the trade periodical in your industry, check out the publication's Web site. Publishers often make some content available for free.

The Internet

It's almost frightening how much information is on the World Wide Web. If you can't make it to your local library or bookstore, visit an online bookstore. What makes these sites so useful for writers are their powerful search functions that allow you to research thousands of books using keywords. When I was researching this book, I went to an online bookstore and did a search for the word "columnists." A list of hundreds of book titles by columnists downloaded before my eyes.

Once you're comfortable logging onto specific sites, try your hand at E-mail, which is useful for making inquiries and interviewing sources;

newsgroups, where you can post a message on what is essentially a community bulletin board; and search engines, such as Lycos and AltaVista, which enable you to locate Web sites related to your topic.

Many columnists operate their own Web sites. The biggest obstacle to running a site, they noted, is the time it takes to keep the site updated, including posting new information, answering E-mails and trying new tactics to keep visitors interested, such as surveys and contests. Chapter nine will explore Web sites in greater detail.

Conferences and Trade Shows

I always try to attend the annual conference of the American Society of Journalists and Authors. It's there that I learn about the latest trends in publishing and what type of material editors are seeking.

As a columnist, you may find yourself attending a lot more than an annual conference. *Ask the Builder* columnist Tim Carter investigates building products for his readers. He says he attends about four trade shows a year, where he learns about the latest products. "At the National Hardware Show alone, there were fifteen hundred new products introduced," he says.

If you can't attend a conference related to your subject, you can learn a lot about it by reading the conference brochure, which you can get for free from the organization sponsoring the event. Most brochures list seminar descriptions, keynote speakers who will talk on a specific trend and vendors attending the show.

From the brochure alone, you can determine the issues at the forefront of attendees' minds. If you spot a seminar speaker addressing a topic you want to know more about, contact that person. The brochure probably won't list the speaker's phone number, but it will almost surely have that person's company name and maybe even the city and state where it's located. From there you can easily get the number. Then call. If you can't get through to the person, ask for her assistant or her E-mail address.

Keep in mind that some conference organizers have their seminars taped, then sell the audiocassettes or videotapes to attendees who couldn't attend. If you purchase taped sessions and use quotes from the tape in your column, be sure to note that the person you quoted was speaking at a seminar. Leading readers to believe you obtained the quotes directly is misleading and unethical. And if you work in a fairly small industry, you may be jeopardizing any opportunity to get an interview with the speaker at a future date.

Press Releases

As an environmental columnist, I made a point of being put on the mailing list of public relations companies representing clients in the environmental field. If you're not receiving press releases, and you'd like to, flip through a trade periodical covering your topic, and note the companies that advertise. Call them and ask to be put on their mailing list for press releases. Though not all companies issue press releases, those that do will more than likely be glad to include you on their list or will refer you to the public relations agency that handles their releases. In many cases, you can receive press releases via E-mail.

Public relations agencies want publicity for their clients and, therefore, are happy to send you material. Unless, that is, they believe you'll use it against them. After all, it's their job to present and maintain favorable images of the companies or institutions they represent.

When calling a company, ask for the public relations, or "P.R.," department. You may be connected with the director of corporate communications, which is basically the same as the public relations director. In addition to providing you with press releases, P.R. staffers may be able to provide you with insight to trends occurring in their industries.

When you start receiving press releases, remember that they are carefully conceived documents whose purpose is to shed positive light on the company or institution they are featuring. Your job is to read between the lines. If it's a new product, try to determine what its implications will be beyond what's stated in the press release. Jot down questions, then call the contact person (usually listed at the top of the release) and begin querying. If you want to talk to the president of the company, you'll still have to go through the public relations person in most cases.

Observation

Entire columns have been written based solely on people observing other people. In *Metropolitan Diary*, a weekly column in *The New York Times*, readers contribute humorous descriptions of everyday life in the city. The column proved so popular that when the paper stopped running it, so many readers complained that it was subsequently reinstated.

You can borrow from this column by learning to observe people and capture in words the conversations and actions that evoke a particular emotion. If you're writing a commentary column on holiday shoppers for your local paper, spend a day observing and listening to shoppers. Note whether the mood is cheery or harried, then capture that mood in your column by describing a conversation you overheard.

These "slices of life" add a strong human element to your column and are often more real and intriguing than straightforward interviews with shoppers. Indeed, what people say and do when they're unaware they're being listened to is often more interesting and humorous than anything they would say if they knew their quotes would appear in print. However, if you use observations in your column, keep the individuals involved in them anonymous.

Experience

Ask the Builder columnist Tim Carter was a contractor before he began writing about home repair and remodeling. "I have hands-on experience about what I write about," he says. "I'm not someone who bought a house and did minor rehabilitation work to it and now thinks he can write a column about it. I was in the trenches for twenty years. I wore a tool belt, got hundreds of stitches and sat on roofs when it was 120° up there. I did all the work, and it shows through in my writing."

While some columnists write from experience, others live what they write about. "I do most of the things I write about," says *The Wild Side* columnist Dr. Scott Shalaway, whose outdoor column focuses on enjoying and learning about nature. "In fact, 90 percent of what I write about is based on my personal experience. I live in the country on ninety-five acres of land. I travel and plant wildflowers. If I get stuck for ideas, I take a walk in the woods."

Surveys

Doing a survey sounds like a formidable undertaking, but it doesn't have to be. It can be an informal verbal survey of your neighbors. Or it can be a survey of people belonging to your favorite chat group. Or it can be a couple of questions tagged onto the survey performed by the editor of the magazine for which you write a column.

This latter idea is doable if you already write features or other occasional pieces for the publication, or the editor likes your column idea but needs more evidence that readers would like it. Ask the editor when she surveys her readers. Most publications survey readers or conduct focus groups to gauge interest in their publications. Ask if you can tag on a couple of questions that will allow you to assess interest in a column you would like to write for the publication.

Start a List

Now that you have a base from which to start cultivating sources and ideas, start two lists, one labeled "sources," the other "topics." Even if you don't have sources at this point, start a file on your computer called "sources," or simply write "sources" on the top of a sheet of paper, and tack it near your work area. Then start adding names of experts you read about, meet and see on television.

Do the same for topics. Create a folder, and as it gets full, section it into subfolders. Old topic ideas can be updated by teaming them with something new, say a recently published book. Some topics never grow old. These are known as "evergreen" topics, because they are always fresh, like the leaves of an evergreen tree. Dieting is an evergreen topic because it can be written about throughout the year, and readers who diet rarely tire of hearing more about the topic. On the other hand, a topic such as purchasing back-to-school supplies is limited to a specific time of year.

Collect enough information on a particular topic, and you can write a trends piece chronicling when the trend began, where it is today and where experts predict it will go. If you don't have a knack for picking up on trends, get into the habit of reading about them in the many books covering the topic. Here are three of them: *Trends 2000: How to Prepare for and Profit From the Changes of the 21st Century; Clicking: 17 Trends That Drive Your Business—and Your Life;* and *Street Trends: How Today's Alternative Youth Cultures Are Creating Tomorrow's Mainstream Markets.*

Review Your Topics

While we're discussing topics and sources, pull out the list of ten column topics that you generated in chapter two. Now expand on them.

Based on what you've read in this chapter, are there new ways to cover any of the topics you've listed? Can you think of sources who would add credibility to a particular column? Can you delete topics that don't seem as topical as they did before? Do you have new ideas that you can substitute? Can you double the number of topics on your list?

A list containing twenty well-thought-out ideas may seem excessive, but it's not. In fact, it may not even be enough. "I get calls from people who want to write columns, and it flummoxes them when you ask them if they have six months to a year's worth of column topics," says *Working Wounded* columnist Bob Rosner. "A lot of people have six or eight ideas and don't realize what it's like to be a long-distance marathoner.

"When [newspaper syndicate] United Feature was interested in picking up my column, they asked me for a list of six months of topic ideas," Rosner continues. "Now I see why they said that, because a lot of people hit a wall. People may have a passion about a topic—photography, cooking—but can you envision yourself at 150 columns? I've written 130."

And, remember, it's not just *how* many topics you generate, but the *quality* of those topics—though, as even veteran columnists can attest, quality is an attribute that is difficult to assess until it's been tested. "Generating topics is like fishing," says *Ask the Builder* columnist Tim Carter. He is able to gauge reader enthusiasm for his topics because each column carries a tag line at the end offering readers "Builder Bulletins," which are printed material that delve into more detail on a topic than can fit in a column.

"I wrote a column about cedar closets," says Carter, "and nationwide, for that 'Builder Bulletin,' I got 80 orders—that's nothing. I get an average of 850 'Bulletin' orders each week.

"When I wrote about concrete, I got so much mail, we could hardly handle it," he continues. "When I wrote a column on synthetic deck sealant, the column generated its largest response—over five thousand requests nationwide for the 'Builder Bulletin' on that topic."

Though columnists have little control over how readers will embrace a topic, they do have control over the topics themselves. When humor columnist and Washington institution Art Buchwald found it difficult to generate new topics for his 400-word, twice-weekly column of political satire that's syndicated in 350 newspapers, the seventy-two-year-old columnist left Washington for New York in part to find new ideas for his column. "After a certain amount of time, there's nothing new," Buchwald stated in a *New York Times* article. "Restaurants are the same, stores are the same, your buddies are the same."

Another, less drastic way to broaden the scope of your column is to expand the range of topics you cover. Such a tactic can be done at any time during the life of a column. One columnist, a Pulitzer Prize finalist, initially focused solely on family and race issues, and said he had to expand the scope of his subject to stay fresh. He now includes women's issues, gay issues and spirituality.

If you decide to expand the scope of your column, be careful not to make it too general. It may become so watered down that it loses its original purpose. Though it's a fine line between covering a subject that's too broad and one that's too specific, rather err on the side of being too specific. You're likelier to get in the door with a narrow subject than a general one, and once you're in, you can always broaden it.

6 Structuring the Column

If you're an auto mechanic, you know all there is to know about fixing cars, and you can spot a scam artist a mile away. If you're a marketing maven, you know how to draw attention to a product. If you're an antique collector, you know the difference between a fake and the real McCoy.

But can you write about it? Possessing the ability to do something well and to write about it clearly and in an interesting way, is a gift—one not shared by many people, but one that can be nurtured and developed.

One way to develop solid writing skills is by writing. That may sound obvious, but too often writers become consumed with learning to write and, consequently, never spend the time actually writing. While interviewing columnists for this book, I came across one who teaches a creative writing course. When asked for advice he could offer aspiring columnists, he reiterated what he says to his students on the first day of class—they would all be better served if they went home and wrote rather than sit in a classroom and try to learn how to write. (He's a humor columnist, so he may have been pulling my leg, but his point is well taken.)

In addition to writing, another way to develop strong writing skills is by reading everything you can get your hands on. I go early to doctors' appointments just to read the magazines. I even subscribe to certain magazines because the writing is terrific, not because I'm interested in the subjects they cover. For example, *Outside* magazine is geared toward men and caters to the interests of outdoor adventurers. Since I'm neither, I normally wouldn't subscribe to this magazine. But the writing is so powerful that I read it to learn how to improve my own writing.

Beyond the more or less obvious ways to develop solid writing skills are several not as well-known and that if followed will almost certainly impress an editor. They are: studying the columns that you believe are well written; learning about the unique aspects of the column format; and avoiding common editorial mistakes that plague new columnists.

Name That Columnist

At this point in your writing, you should be familiar with columnists whose work you admire. They do not have to be writers who cover the same subject as you do in your column. But their work should include elements that you value, whether it's a particular writing style or the way the column is structured.

When asked to name their favorite columnists, the columnists I interviewed didn't hesitate. In fact, some of them had even contacted their favorite columnists to express their admiration and to ask for advice regarding their own column-writing careers. If someone were to ask you to name your favorite columnists, could you cite two or three?

If your favorite columnists do not include your competition, then make a point of observing the work of columnists with whom your columns compete. The columnists I talked to were well aware of their competitors, and it's important to note that they respected them. Indeed, never disparage your competitor's work. It's a sign of an unprofessional, insecure writer, and few editors want to work with someone like that.

Ask the Builder columnist Tim Carter said he was aware of an aspiring columnist who is "about a year away from doing what I'm doing." In response, Carter is developing new products and ideas that he believes will "make it impossible for him, and anyone else, to get started." This may sound excessive, but this columnist has turned column writing into a full-time career that pays him handsomely, and he's not about to give up his turf. (For the complete interview with Tim Carter, please see pages 107-109.)

When studying the work of your competitors, note how your column differs from theirs. You'll use this information when selling your idea to editors. That's because in column writing, there are few—if any—new subjects to cover. But there are new ways to cover old subjects, and this is an important key to realizing your dream of becoming a published columnist.

Perhaps you write about people who run their own businesses, and another columnist also covers that subject. However, your column has a niche, focusing on teenagers who have developed their own part-time businesses. An editor looking to attract younger readers to her publication would likely jump at the chance to run your work. She may even pay you well to prevent you from trying to sell your work to the publication that competes against hers.

Content and Structure

OK, so you've gotten your hands on some columns by a writer who covers a subject that you want to cover. How do you study them, and what can you learn from them? There are two elements to examine: content and structure.

The content is the main substance of a piece of writing. It includes such elements as how facts are presented and how the piece is organized, the writer's attitude, how he approached the topic and whether he reached a conclusion. If you've ever felt let down after having read a column, that means its content was weak. If you've ever read a column that stayed in your mind for days afterward, then the content was strong.

When reading a column for content, note whether the column is backed up with research. Does it contain quotes that are attributed to specific people? Or, is the writer less formal, seldom bothering to identify someone quoted? Does the column ramble on, or does it maintain a focus on one specific topic? These ingredients determine a column's content.

One way to study content is to put yourself in the writer's mind and visualize his thought process when he wrote the column. Editors do this every day. Before they edit an article or a column, editors read it through. Then they try to determine why the writer wrote the piece the way he did. Such an exercise helps you uncover writing techniques that make a column come to life, and it enables you to apply those techniques to your own writing to make your columns sharper, more focused and entertaining.

Now note the structure of the columns you're studying. Does the writer use short or long sentences, or a combination of both? Does the column consist of straight text, or is it sectioned into different parts? Perhaps it starts with a question-and-answer format, then features a book review and concludes with a quote from an attributed source.

With the trend toward shorter columns, it's more important than ever for you to pay attention to the structure, or format, of columns. Today's columnists have fewer words in which to make their points. So before you start to write your column, know how it will be structured.

Another way to study structure is to separate the column into parts: the introduction, the middle and the conclusion. Notice how writers start their columns, how they maintain readers' attention throughout the middle of the column and how they reward readers for completing the column in its entirety. Let's look at each element in detail.

In the Beginning

From chapter four, you know that strong headlines and callouts draw readers into a column. But they only draw readers as far as the first sentence. Moving them beyond that first sentence requires a great introduction, which is also known as a lead, an opener or a hook (because it "hooks" readers into wanting more). To avoid confusion, I'll refer to the introduction as the opener.

A well-written opener draws in readers whether or not they are interested in the topic of the overall column. I'm not in sales, nor am I particularly interested in selling, but I was immediately drawn to this business column, which opened with the following paragraph:

> The only thing worse than a pushy salesman in a slick suit is a salesman *pushing* a slick suit. In 1973, that insight led George Zimmer to open a store that would sell suits differently from how they'd been sold before.
>
> (from *Fast Company* magazine, "They Sell Suits With Soul" by Eric Ransdell)

Do I care how a store called Men's Wearhouse sells business suits? No, but because of this lead, I continued reading.

In addition to using clever plays on words, opening a column with an anecdote is another way to draw in readers. Consider this biographical anecdote:

> It happened so fast, I had no time to react. The squirrel darted in front of my car and—blotto! I felt sick. "Just a squirrel," some might say, but every roadkill is an unfortunate death.
>
> (from *The Wild Side* by Dr. Scott Shalaway)

A common mistake columnists make is hiding a great opener two or three paragraphs down into the column. Read your past columns, and note if you have a tendency to do this. It's not unusual for a columnist to unintentionally write two paragraphs of bland copy before shifting into high gear.

By the third paragraph, the columnist generates clear, readable, interesting copy.

If you tend to write this way, write long—meaning, exceed the word count you've set for yourself or your editor has set for you. Then edit your column, searching for the opener further down in your copy. Chances are it's lying there waiting to be discovered.

More often than not, a weak opener is the result of laziness, not lack of skill. For example, while there is nothing technically wrong with opening a column with a question, it shows little creativity and won't draw in readers. If you're writing a pet column about how to give a cat a bath, opening with the question "Do you know how to give your cat a bath?" probably won't draw in many readers. Sure, those who have been looking for the answer to this particular question will read the column, but few others will. As a columnist, you want to draw in readers who don't even own cats.

If you tend to open your columns with questions, don't despair. Such a column can be easily improved by deleting the question and making some simple edits to the text following it. Say I was writing my pet column, and I had written:

> Do you know how to give your cat a bath? I didn't until my cat smelled so bad he didn't need a bell around his neck to alert me to his presence. I could smell him before I could see him. It was then I decided to learn the basics of cat bathing.

By deleting the question and doing some minor editing, the opener is definitely strengthened:

> My cat smelled so bad he didn't need a bell around his neck to alert me to his presence. I could smell him before I could see him. It was then I decided to learn the basics of cat bathing.

If you want to notify readers early on that the column will cover how to give a cat a bath, write a headline that reflects the topic, such as "Baths for Cats Made Easy," or "These Bathing Techniques Are the Cat's Meow." Though there is no guarantee that the editor will use the headline, your opener is so clever that even if the editor replaces your headline with a bland one, the column will still attract lots of readers.

A Solid Middle

A great opener is important, but it alone won't carry readers through your column. To do that you need to maintain reader interest by offering more, which in this case is information that builds on the opener.

Often referred to as the "nuts and bolts" of the column, the middle section of a column provides readers with information that relates to the purpose of the column. For example, if you write a martial arts column and one particular column focuses on self-defense, the middle might provide readers with techniques to ward off an attacker. If you write a computer column and are focusing on the topic of avoiding crashes, the middle of the column could provide readers with specific tips for avoiding a crash.

A word of advice: Just because you drew in readers with a clever opener doesn't mean you can't handle the middle of the column in an equally interesting way. While providing readers with the facts about a particular topic, think about how to add spark to the writing.

Take the cat bathing example. The opener hooked readers into wanting to read about how to give a cat a bath. Now you have to actually tell them how to do it. Listing step-by-step instructions is one way to do it, and there's nothing technically wrong with this technique. However, it probably won't carry most readers all the way through the column.

Why not try sprinkling a series of humorous asides throughout the instructions? (After all, bathing cats isn't such a serious topic that you, and your readers, can't have fun with it.) If the first step is to fill the kitchen sink with warm water, you might add an aside such as:

> Pretend you're about to wash your cat's food dish, and wonder aloud "Once I get this dish cleaned, I can fill it with Fluffy's favorite food." This will serve two purposes: to fill the sink with water and to trick Fluffy into entering the kitchen when she normally wouldn't come ten feet within the sound of running water.

Even if I didn't own a cat, I would read this column just for a laugh. Since the column is not only humorous, but provides useful information, I might even clip it and mail or fax it to a friend who owns a cat. Who knows? Maybe my friend would mail it to the editor of her local paper, noting that the paper should run such a column. Certainly, stranger things have happened.

A Perfect Ending

The ending, or conclusion, should reward the reader for having read the column in its entirety. The ending not only sums up the column, but should leave readers eagerly anticipating the next one.

There are two ways to end a column: with a bang or a thud. Too often, writers don't bother concluding their column, or they write a final paragraph that boringly summarizes what the column has covered. Both amount to large-scale thuds to an editor and readers.

Just like the cup of coffee that's "good to the last drop," a column ought to be interesting to the last word. Admittedly, the concluding paragraph is difficult to write. After writing an exciting lead and working hard to draw readers into the meat of the column, columnists are tired by the end. If the word count is running short, it's tempting to tag on a concluding paragraph that's neat, accurate and, unfortunately, boring. If the word count is long, the columnist might be tempted to stop writing, leaving the column with no conclusion.

If you've taken the time and energy to write a thoughtful lead and a solid middle, why not follow through and end the column on an equally strong note? Certainly, readers deserve a payoff for reading the column in its entirety. If the ending is weak, they may not read your next column.

A tried-and-true way to end a column is with a strong quote. The quote shouldn't raise questions, since at this point, you're ending the column. Rather, it should reinforce the point of the column. But it can do so in several ways: by adding an element of surprise, ending on a humorous note or relating to the opener in a way that brings the column full circle.

Using the cat bathing column example, you might try the latter technique and end the column with the following paragraph:

> Fluffy is clean. In fact, she's so clean, I've had to put a bell around her neck so I know when she's coming.

This concluding paragraph brings the column full circle because it clearly relates to the opener. Such a technique also carries the humorous tone throughout the entire column.

Another way to conclude your column is to provide readers with additional information. If you write a travel column, you can end it by providing telephone numbers where readers can get more information on the destination discussed in your column. Or instead of providing more information, ask readers to submit information to you. For example, if you write about white-water rafting, you might end the column by requesting that readers send in their experiences navigating these types of waters so you can share them with everyone in your next column.

Though there are lots of creative ways to end a column, don't forget that sometimes a simple, one-sentence ending works well, too. A nature column that delves into the topic of acorns might end with this simple sentence: "That's the story of the acorn—in a nutshell."

Avoiding Common Mistakes

As you've seen, the column format is not as easy to master as it looks. In a short amount of space, columnists must excite, spur to action or entertain readers. Run-on sentences, evasive language and long introductions eat up valuable editorial space.

Being aware of editorial mistakes commonly found in columns is the first step to avoiding them. Following are mistakes I frequently encounter when editing columns:

Inaccuracies

As a columnist, you are the expert, and readers and editors expect you to be correct. If you don't know the answer to a question or aren't sure about a particular fact, you know who to turn to for the answer.

And when you turn to another expert for advice, identify that person by name, and check the spelling of that person's name. Don't leave that chore for your editor, who may not have the time to check it.

If you really want to endear yourself to your editor, provide the editor with backup material that verifies that the information in your column is correct. For example, if you visit an online bookstore to double-check the title and author of a book mentioned in your column, print out the page containing the information, and turn it in with your column. You'll have saved your editor fifteen minutes checking it herself.

Vagueness

You're writing your column, and you want to include information you re-member reading in a book, but you can't remember the title of the book, so you write "According to a book I recently read. . . ." Not good enough.

As a columnist, you'll only frustrate readers this way. Same goes for identifying people in your column. Using the nonspecific phrase "According to sources . . ." is not acceptable. Unless you're William Safire, and people know you have well-connected contacts whom you can't name, you cannot get away with such weak reporting methods.

Redundancies

Redundancies result when writers repeat information already stated. The rule is: Say it well once. If there is something especially interesting you want to convey to readers, say it and move on. This is especially important when it comes to columns, where redundancies are more noticeable to readers than in longer pieces of writing.

Poor, or No, Transitions

A transition is a passage that moves the reader from one paragraph to the next. An effective transition gives a column cohesiveness and logic. It might be achieved by merely adding one word, such as *but*, as in:

> I didn't get the job.
> But I did get a tip on another position.

Such an editorial device alerts readers to a change in the mood from the previous sentence and thus avoids confusion. Other transitional words include *yet, however, nevertheless, still, instead, thus, therefore, meanwhile, now* and *later*.

Missing Information

It's typical for a columnist to write long, then edit the copy down to the proper word count. But what often happens during this editing process is that information pertaining to the remaining copy gets deleted, resulting in a column that raises more questions than it answers.

To avoid this, make a point of reading the column through each time you cut a chunk of it—even if it's only half a sentence. Though this type of problem is more common in longer pieces, it does occur in columns and is a sure sign of a writer's inattentiveness to her work.

Incomplete Information

There's nothing more frustrating to a reader than to be given partial information. If you mention the title of a book, give readers information that will help them find the book. Supply the author's name and the complete title of the book. If space allows, include the publisher.

Similarly, if you include in your column the name of a company, include the city and state where it's located. By providing this information, readers can call directory assistance and get the company's phone number. If your readers are likely to be computer literate, supply the company's Web site address.

Long Sentences

Because the column format is short, it follows that the paragraphs and sentences within columns should also be short. Try "writing short" on your next column. It's easy. Right away, you'll notice the powerful punch short sentences deliver.

Consider the first three sentences of this column about swimming holes:

> We call it "The Rock." It is where my father taught my brothers and me to swim. But the name misleads.

Three short sentences that propel readers to want to continue. Less noticeable, but as important, is the way these simple sentences capture the feeling one associates with childhood memories.

Punctuation

Correct punctuation works magic on a column. It adds clarity, emotion and rhythm (yes, columns should sound pleasing to readers' ears). When used incorrectly, punctuation muddies the column, thus distracting the reader.

Common punctuation mistakes include excessive use of exclamation marks, which causes them to lose their effectiveness. (Some experts caution writers to avoid using exclamation marks altogether.)

Dashes and commas are also often overused. I've seen columns containing so many dashes and commas, it's difficult to tell where a sentence begins and where it ends. I've seen semicolons used when a colon would have been more appropriate and parentheses used when commas would have done just fine.

If you don't know how to punctuate, invest a few dollars in at least one book on punctuation. Here are a few to choose from: *Punctuation Marks* by Martha Coaxum Hodrick (1998); *Webster's New World Notebook*

Grammar & Punctuation Guide, edited by John A. Haslem, Jr. (1998); and *Pocket Guide to Punctuation and Style* (1998).

Unnecessary Words

There are certain words that, though not technically incorrect, serve only to dilute copy. Some of those words are *obviously*, *of course*, *naturally*, *currently* and *personally*. If something is obvious, you don't have to state it. Try reading your sentence without the word *currently* or *personally*. Chances are the sentence will work without it.

Granted, sometimes these words work well in commentary column writing, where the writer is trying to be humorous or impart a particular voice. But overall, they are redundant or serve only to introduce text that doesn't enhance the column.

Misuse of Statistics

I used to believe that statistics lent an air of professionalism to a column—until I read a book by Darrell Huff called *How to Lie With Statistics*. Though woefully outdated in terms of the language and examples it uses (it was published in 1954), it clearly illustrates how statistics can be manipulated to make practically any point.

With that said, don't take statistics at their face value. Look at where they came from and how they are presented. If you do cite statistics in your column, name their source. That way, readers can judge for themselves whether they deem them reliable.

Unclear Purpose

If after reading halfway through a column, the reader finds herself asking, "What's the point?" you know the column lacks a purpose. Anyone who spends her time reading a column doesn't want to finish with more questions than the column answers.

Before writing, make sure you know what you want to write about. Settle on one point you want to make, and stay focused on that.

Few or No Breaks in the Text

Not all columns have to be straight text. They can contain bulleted lists, letters from readers and other elements. Such devices break up the text and make it easier to read, thereby enticing readers to spend time with the column.

Working Wounded columnist Bob Rosner inserts as many as five different elements in his weekly 500-word column: a letter containing a work-related problem, his response to the letter, an excerpt from a recently published business book, a "List of the Week" containing statistics or other relevant information and contest instructions. Not only does this structure make reading the column easier, according to Rosner, it "gives people a home that feels familiar every week."

7 Engaging Your Audience

If editors knew what made for engaging columns, the column-writing business would be a fairly uncreative profession. Editors would hand columnists step-by-step instructions, and perhaps even a fill-in-the-blank form, and columnists would simply follow the drill.

Fortunately, that's not the case. Editors are rarely 100 percent sure of who is reading a particular column and the degree to which readers find it engaging. That's what makes column writing so fascinating.

When it comes to a column's "core" readership, editors do have general facts—median household income and level of education, for example. Core readers are those loyal fans who read every column and are usually involved in what the column covers. If it's a recipe column, core readers test those recipes in their kitchens. If it's a travel column, core readers visit the destinations described in the column. If it's a craft column, core readers create the projects outlined in the column.

Then there are "periphery" readers. Periphery readers may glance at the column, noting the headline and callout, and perhaps read the first paragraph. Sometimes they read it through its entirety because the topic interests them or because a previous column proved enjoyable. But the subject of the column is one that, on the whole, isn't near and dear to them. Still, periphery readers can make up a substantial portion of a columnist's audience.

Take Ron Shaffer's *Dr. Gridlock* column, which runs in *The Washington Post*, and was one of the first commuter columns in the United States. His core readership is, of course, commuters. However, periphery readers also make up a strong faction, as the writer himself described in an October 24, 1998, *Editor & Publisher* article: "Even people who aren't affected [by traffic] like reading the column because it's, like, 'Oh, wow! I don't have to do that!'"

Periphery readers are often drawn into a column for reasons that go beyond its subject. Oftentimes, it's the right mix of several ingredients, such as voice, style *and* content. When all three components hit the mark, you have a column that is engaging and entertaining—often regardless of the subject it covers. When even one element is off, you've missed an opportunity to draw in periphery readers and to leave a lasting impression on your loyal core readers.

Skilled editors have an ear and eye for the editorial elements that make up a column. "I look for a lead that grabs me, one basic theme, no cliches, no 'holier-than-thou' attitude and an ending that leaves me thinking," said *The Miami Herald* assistant managing editor/features Elissa Vanaver in an October 31, 1998, *Editor & Publisher* article.

But most editors—whether due to time restraints or skill levels—will not try to improve upon a columnist's voice and style, change the column's content or rewrite an opener or conclusion. For the most part, editors do not have the time to delve into a column beyond rewriting a headline, editing the copy to fit the space allotted to it and fixing typos and grammatical errors. And they shouldn't have to, because voice, style and content are the job of the writer.

The Good, the Bad and the Ugly

You want to get into the habit of editing your work not only because it's your responsibility, but because, as in any profession, the quality of editors runs the gamut from good to bad to the just plain old ugly. I've worked with editors who would go to extremes to reach a columnist to make a small clarification. I've worked with editors whose only concern was that the column fit the space allotted to it. And I've worked with editors whose intentions were good, but unfortunately, the same couldn't be said of their skills.

Certainly, it's not unheard of for columnists not to recognize their work after it's been edited. Writing in *Brill's Content* magazine, New York journalism instructor Susan Shapiro lamented that editors changed her copy so much she could hardly recognize her own words. In one op-ed column, she noted that editors deleted references to her shoplifting exploits as a child. "I deduced that you're not allowed to commit a crime on the op-ed page," she wrote.

Working Wounded columnist Bob Rosner is also no stranger to the editor's heavy hand. He recounts an episode when a newspaper editor cut 150 words from his 500-word humor/business column to fit it into a different slot in the paper. To make matters worse, according to Rosner, the newspaper "found the least funny person on its staff and cut out virtually every joke."

Rosner's reaction was to move his column to a competing newspaper. "You have to be open to being edited, but you also have to draw a line," he says.

Rosner had the luxury of being able to take his work to a competing paper that readily accepted it. You will probably not have that luxury in the early stages of your column-writing career. Therefore, since your column may initially be picked up by just one publication, make a point of getting to know your editor. Take her out to lunch, and ask her what she feels makes for a strong column, how she edits columns and how you could improve your column.

And don't rely just on editors. *Working Wounded* columnist Bob Rosner noted that when he was picked up by a newspaper syndicate, one of the salesmen there provided helpful information. He not only gave Rosner insight into the syndication business, but he helped him improve his writing voice, better position himself in the subject category in which he writes and suggested adding two elements to the column that Rosner eventually included.

If you know an editor, ask that person to read your columns and provide input. If you don't know an editor, consider a friend or spouse. Two of the columnists interviewed for this book noted that at one point in their column-writing careers, their wives edited their columns.

If your "editor" doesn't mind, ask if you may observe him reading your column. One way to tell if you've written an engaging column is to assess its emotional impact. At some point in the column, a reader should exhibit a change of mood or emotion—a smile, a burst of laughter, anger or raised eyebrows—an indication that the text somehow moved them. If you can provoke this type of passion, you're more likely to win readers' hearts and minds.

In addition to having someone read your column, establish a method for editing your column, then stick to it. And don't be surprised if you spend as much, or more, time editing your column as you do writing it.

Bob Rosner developed a method of editing that results in his revising his columns up to thirty-eight times. "I always have six columns at varying stages," he says. "I have my most recent column, which I've gone over and over to get right. The next week's column is less well edited, and so on. I never go directly to the last column. I always go to the most recent one, edit it, then edit the next one. All the columns I'm working on have had thirty to thirty-eight edits on them.

"This technique allows me to get in a mind-set and refine my columns," he continues. "It has eliminated 'blank screen disease,' where you sit in front of your computer screen. It sounds compulsive, but when you're a columnist, you must have a distinctive voice, and you must achieve that on a regular basis."

What Is Voice?

Anyone who read a newspaper in the 1970s and 1980s is familiar with the so-called "urban columnists," such as Mike Royko, Jimmy Breslin and Herb Caen. These writers translated for the public at large the feelings of workers and immigrants in the country's large cities. Few who read those columns weren't touched by them.

For these columnists, their voices were everything. You could read an urban column and know who wrote it without looking at the byline. But when city dwellers began migrating to suburbia and rural areas, it became increasingly difficult for a handful of columnists to speak for an increasingly fragmented society. In addition, the growth of the Internet as a source of information, as well as the increase in the number of television news programs, made it more difficult for urban columnists to be heard.

As a result of these changes, some urban voices migrated to talk radio and cable television. In addition, instead of relying on one voice to represent their cities, newspapers hired several urban columnists with different backgrounds.

The voice of the urban columnist had become irrelevant to its audience. It no longer engaged readers because those readers had changed. As the audience for urban columns changed, so did urban columnists, who now represented new populations of immigrants and infused newspapers with a fresh voice. For aspiring columnists, this change represented an opportunity.

What makes developing a voice so difficult is the fact that readers' tastes change throughout the years. Read a column from several decades ago and the writing may sound forced and awkward compared to the natural voice of today's columnists.

Exercise

Choose five adjectives that describe the voice of your column. Is it sassy, plaintive, wise, emphatic, inspiring, passionate? Does the voice of your column speak to the audience you envision reading your column? Learning to connect your voice to that of your audience lends your work a consistency that encourages readers to return.

Natural and Distinctive

Whether you write about business travel one week and home cooking the next, readers should be able to identify you by your writing voice. If your voice is natural, as it should be, they will. In fact, a good writing voice has been likened to the writer speaking to the reader over coffee at the kitchen table. You *want* readers to recognize you as much by your writing voice as those who know you personally recognize you by the sound of your voice.

"Writers need more distinctive voices," says Rosner. "I think there is a huge need for good writing and a huge need for columns. But to be a good storyteller week after week is tough, and there's not a lot out there. I've probably gotten sixty E-mails from people who tell me I'm the first thing they read when they pick up the paper. It's touching: The phenomena when you pick up a paper and don't just leaf through it but have a destination. That's a phenomena that should happen a lot."

Though writers' voices differ, there are several common steps you can take to strengthen yours. They are:

• Use the active voice. The active voice is usually more direct and vigorous than the passive voice. The active voice makes a sentence stronger, and consequently, tightens it, making it easier to read: "John threw the ball" (active voice) versus "The ball was thrown by John" (passive voice).

• Stick to one topic. The topic refers to the person, group, place, thing, incident or issue in a column. Many magazine pieces have a main topic and a subtopic that deepens the story. Due to length constrictions, columns should stick to one topic. Trying to inject additional elements dilutes the column and may confuse readers.

• Point out your own foibles, mistakes and weaknesses. Having your name and words appear in print on a regular basis elevates writers in some readers' minds to celebrity status. Noting your human frailties will put you on the same level as your audience, which is right where you want to be.

• Develop an ear for good writing. Read your column aloud. It should have its own tempo and rhythm, as though you're reading a poem. Sentences should flow into one another, and paragraphs should transition smoothly. By developing an ear for good writing, you improve the sound of your writing voice.

What Is Style?

Once you identify and develop your writing voice, start to work on your style. Though an elusive concept, style refers to a writer's unique way of presenting and expressing his ideas. Though style is often inherent, it can be improved on by practicing writing and mastering grammatical techniques.

For many writers, style is hidden beneath overwriting. Veteran columnists have perfected the art of whittling down their writing to its bare bones while maintaining their style. It's an art, and it takes time to learn, but once mastered, it pays off. When readers spend time with a column written by a longtime columnist, they're often hardly aware that they're reading. Instead, they're transferred to the place about which they're reading. It's that kind of seduction you want to create in every column.

Exercise

Read two or three of your columns and judge whether they sound the way you sound when you're speaking in a comfortable setting. Oftentimes, a writer—especially one working under a tight deadline—will come off as stiff and authoritative rather than relaxed and confident.

To develop style, you've got to be yourself, and to be yourself, you must relax and have confidence, according to William Zinsser, author of the classic nonfiction writing guide *On Writing Well*. However, that's easier said than done.

"Telling a writer to relax is like telling a man to relax while being examined for a hernia," Zinsser writes in his book, "and as for confidence, see how stiffly he sits, glaring at the screen that awaits his words. See how often he gets up to look for something to eat or drink. A writer will do anything to avoid the act of writing. I can testify from my newspaper days that the number of trips to the water cooler per reporter-hour far exceeds the body's need for fluids."

If any advice for developing a sound style can be offered, it's that writers should strive for simplicity. No overstatements. No cliches. No putting on airs. No embellishing. Just good, basic writing—finding the right words to describe the topic and believing you have something worth saying.

Find Your Niche

Engaging an audience in your column is sometimes as straightforward as matching a publication's audience to what you believe they would like to read. Readers of the newspaper covering your part of suburbia may very well want to read your slice-of-life column about your experiences living there. A cooking magazine might welcome a column in which you review the latest kitchen gadgets.

But readers' interests can often be surprising. Sometimes they're interested in exactly the opposite of what you would think. Some conservatives want to read about the views of liberals and vice versa. Readers of baby magazines, which are generally read by more women than men, might welcome a column from a new father's perspective. And perhaps a magazine that covers life in the country wants to hear from a city dweller on his take of life in the country.

Indeed, sometimes a column that seems an illogical fit for a publication excels for that very reason. When in 1982 the conservative *Detroit News* launched a weekly column about life from a gay perspective, it seemed an unlikely match. But sixteen years later, the column's author, Deb Price, is still writing her column for the paper. Part of what makes the column so appealing to a large varied audience is Price's writing style—breezy, upbeat, neither defensive nor hostile. Take the opening of this column:

> There's no confusion when a woman says: "This is my husband." But how do I introduce the woman I've lived with for six years to my boss?
>
> Is she my "girlfriend" or my "significant other"? My "longtime companion" or my "lover"?

And though general humor columns have long been used in newspapers to offset hard news stories, it wasn't always common to find business columns laced with humor. Perhaps that's why Bob Rosner's column has proved so popular in newspaper business sections where it offsets the newsy, serious tone of articles found there. Consider this *Working Wounded* column that answers a reader's question about co-workers who lie:

> Consider Julia Genuse, listed in the *Guinness Book of World Records* for having the most tattoos. Some 95 percent of her body is covered with colored ink! People who pass her on the street probably assume she's making a statement with all that art. But the simple truth is that Julia has a skin disease and the tattoos help keep her skin from blistering. Well, just as there's an underlying reason for all the surface art on Julia, there might be a below-the-surface reason your co-worker let you down. Before you end your relationship—or your

job—I suggest you do a little probing. Check out the book *Reading People* (Random House, 1998) by Jo-Ellan Dimitrius, a former O.J. Simpson jury consultant. Dimitrius' tips are as relevant at work as they are in the courtroom. . . .

Some columnists have made names for themselves by appealing to a largely ignored audience. For example, few columnists wrote about life in the suburbs until about ten years ago when William Geist did so for the *Chicago Tribune*. Today, his style is instantly recognizable for its solid reporting techniques combined with humor and insight, as in the introduction to this column:

> Millions of suburban Americans are being deprived of the full status, satisfaction and reward of suburban living because their neighborhoods and subdivisions do not have names.

As in Geist's column, personal essays work best when readers can readily relate to the topic, such as traffic jams described here by *The Road Warrior* columnist Jeffrey Page:

> There are indignities everyone bears, such as inhaling carbon monoxide fumes in a traffic jam on a steamy day in summer.

And, yes, there are times when a straightforward, no-nonsense column works, as in this instructional, or "how-to," column by Dorsey Connors called *Helpful Hints*:

> The joyous holidays can be marred if they are not planned and organized well in advance. Here are tips to help you to do that.

Here, the column opens with a short introduction, then immediately jumps into the meat of the column, which in this case consists of ways to organize holiday chores. But just because a how-to column's number one purpose is to be instructional, doesn't mean it can't contain a strong human element, as in this fitness column:

> Exercising with your significant other can be a wonderful, rewarding experience. It can be advantageous in motivation and can create

consistency in your program. On the other hand, it could pave the road to hell and provide you with ammunition for a war.

So go out there and find your editorial niche. Then fill it with your unique voice and style. That's one strategy for engaging an audience that has never changed.

PART THREE

Selling the Column

8 Submitting to a Publication

The quality of your columns should speak for themselves. But in the real world, editors need more. They want to know why they should run your column, who is likely to read it, what people will gain from reading it and why you are qualified to write it. That information and more is contained in a "pitch," or "query," letter that you will send, along with several sample columns, to an editor.

The amount of sample columns you should send depends on the frequency of your column. If you plan to approach a monthly magazine, a selection of six sample columns should suffice. Six columns is enough to give an editor an idea of your writing style, your approach to your subject and whether your style complements the editor's publication.

If you're proposing a weekly column, be prepared to submit more than six columns. Though you will initially submit six, if an editor is interested in your work, he may request more. After all, six columns represent only a week and a half worth of work.

Since a great deal of territory has been covered so far, it's important that you have everything in order. Before writing your pitch letter, review the following checklist. It summarizes key points made in previous chapters. Making sure you've covered the items in the checklist will strengthen your overall proposal.

Pitch Letter Checklist

❏ You know why you want to write a column—for personal satisfaction, financial opportunity or both—and have set an appropriate time frame for achieving those goals.

❏ You've determined the type of column you want to write, and each one delivers what it promises. For example, if you write a humorous business advice column, each column offers practical work-related tips presented in an amusing manner.

❏ You've researched the markets, including newspapers, magazines and Web sites, and know which publications within those markets would be most receptive to your work.

❏ You're familiar with the editorial format—word counts and the use of callouts, sidebars and bios—of the publication you've targeted.

❏ You have a list of at least twenty topics, and you could develop another twenty without much difficulty.

❏ Those topics can be backed up with facts, statistics and quotes from sources you have developed.

❏ The content and structure of your column is as strong as it can be, and the voice and style capture the essence of what you're trying to convey.

❏ The opening paragraph of each column would make potential readers want to read on.

❏ The middle portion of your columns tackles the topic head on, providing readers with useful information delivered in an entertaining way.

❏ The concluding paragraph of each column brings readers full circle, neatly and creatively summing up the topic discussed.

❏ You've found an "editor" who provides objective criticism of your work, whether that person is a real editor or someone whose judgment you value.

❏ You've invested in a grammar book and refer to it whenever you have a related question.

❏ You have at least six polished columns.

The Tell-All Title

Before you start writing your pitch letter, let's look at an element of your column we haven't explored: its title. The title is not the same as a headline, which we explored in chapter four. Headlines differ for each column; the title of a column remains the same—like the title of a book.

An effective title reflects the subject of the overall column, such as an opinion column called *My Turn*. It should appeal to the column's intended audience and position you as someone whose work is worth reading—no small feat in today's crowded column market. Consider the following column titles:

- *The Virtual Woman: A Woman's Weekly Guide to Cyberspace*. This column picks up on the trend toward more women using the Internet by providing Web sites that would appeal to them.
- *Travel the Net*. The Internet continues to play a leading role in new columns. Here, Joe Harkins reviews travel Web sites and Internet services in this weekly column.
- *The Jungle*. In its weekly employment section, the *Wall Street Journal* rolled out this column on executive pay and recruitment. Upon launching the column, managing editor Paul Steiger said, "The scramble to recruit and retain talent is a terrific story that I want to see us cover even more extensively."
- *Amish Cook*. Elizabeth Coblentz, a sixty-one-year-old Amish woman, handwrites this weekly syndicated column by lantern light. Her ability to offer a glimpse into an old-time lifestyle that's usually private has charmed many readers. In fact, newspapers were reluctant to buy a column they felt was unsophisticated, but numerous readers made their feelings known to editors, and today it runs in more than fifty newspapers in twelve states.
- *Grillings*. Jonathan Lansner, business columnist for the *Orange County Register*, pens this monthly column on the fast-food business.
- *700 Words*. John Boston, an award-winning humor/commentary columnist, self-syndicates this 700-word column, which he writes for *The Signal* (Santa Clarita, California).

A strong title captures the gist of the column and is as memorable as it is clever. It entices potential readers by identifying a problem and offering help with that problem—even if the "problem" is only the need for a little humor or help with a craft project.

A title should also instill curiosity and set the tone for the column. *The Mature Traveler* indicates a serious column for seniors; *Working Wounded* conveys a business advice column sprinkled with humor; *The Wild Side* indicates an insightful and informative look at nature; *Ask the Builder* conveys a serious advice column related to home improvement; and *Roadside Attractions Along the Information Highway* plays on the term "information highway," while indicating that the column will provide readers with interesting Web sites.

These titles work because they reveal the subject of the column and the approach it takes, *and* they use words in a clever way. Many column titles

85

fall short because they accomplish only the first two goals. The problem with using a witty title is that there's a fine line between enticing readers into a column with the title and confusing them to the point where they turn the page. That's where subtitles come in.

If the title of your column is clever, but doesn't go far enough in revealing the subject of the column, consider tagging on a subtitle. A subtitle is a second title that clarifies the main title, as in *Working Wounded: Advice That Adds Insight to Injury*. Here, the subtitle clarifies the title and alerts readers to the fact that the column offers advice. It also incorporates an amusing play on the saying "to add insult to injury."

Though an editor may drop your subtitle, it's a good idea to develop one if the title of your column is vague. You can use the subtitle in your pitch letter to clarify to the editor the subject of your column.

Tools of the Trade

Now it's time to replace your writer's hat with your sales and marketing hat, because you're almost ready to write a pitch letter that will accompany your six columns. Before you outline your letter, however, make sure you have the proper tools.

Today's computers are relatively inexpensive. It pays to have one because many editors prefer columns be submitted on a disk or by E-mail. This saves editors the time-consuming task of having to key in the material themselves. Indeed, Elizabeth Coblentz is one of the few columnists who can get away with handwriting her weekly syndicated column *Amish Cook*.

Editors will often request a "hard copy" of your column as well. Hard copy refers to the printed version of your column—something that will look more professional if it's printed on a high-quality laser printer.

If you don't own a computer or a high-quality laser printer, check out your local library. Most make available to patrons good quality computers and printers, though they often attach a time limit to their use. Still, the quality will impress an editor and position you as a professional.

Also, pay attention to the stationery you use. Plain white or off-white bond paper is best, as opposed to perforated paper or stationery with busy or unnecessary designs. If you've designed a logo for your column, don't include it with your work. I've rarely seen logos run with columns, and including one may lessen your level of professionalism in the eyes of an editor.

Use the reference works described in the Resources section to find the name of the appropriate editor to whom you should address your proposal.

Sometimes you can find the editor's name by referring to the masthead in the publication you wish to submit to or on the publication's Web site.

Making Your Pitch

Writing a pitch letter is like writing an advertisement for your column. It should be geared toward a particular editor at a particular publication, and it should convince the editor to buy your column. Therefore, put as much into writing your pitch letter as you put into your columns. To that extent, your letter should be clear, accurate, enticing and short—no more than one or two single-spaced pages.

All pitch letters contain similar elements. By examining each of these elements separately, you'll have an easier time writing yours.

• *Pitch letters open with a "hook" intended to lure an editor with your first few words.* A hook can be an eye-opening statistic or a dramatic human situation. If I was proposing a column titled *Simply Living* that detailed how to live a physically and mentally uncluttered life, either of these two hooks would be appropriate:

> A full 82 percent of eight hundred Americans agreed with the statement, "We buy far more than we need," according to the results of a phone survey performed by Merck Family Fund.

> "Voluntary simplicity" is one of the major trends leading into the twenty-first century, according to the Trends Research Institute.

Note that I identified the sources of these statistics. Editors and readers need to know where statistics come from to assess whether they are believable. While you don't have to describe the source itself since you are limited to one or two pages, provide the name of the organization that performed the research.

If you can't find statistics that illustrate your point, use an anecdote that puts a human spin on the subject:

> Mary walked carefully from her Suburban, juggling two large packages in one hand and two more in the other, purchases she neither needed nor could afford. As she stepped into her house, her first thought was, "What do I have to throw out in order to make room for these things?"

Hooks that use a human situation may be invented, unlike those that utilize statistics. But they should illustrate situations to which most people can relate.

Notice that the longer hook is still only two sentences in length. Don't waste valuable space drawing out a lengthy anecdote. Wordiness is not a trait valued by editors.

• *Pitch letters describe who will want to read your column.* By noting that there is an established market for your column, editors gain confidence about publishing it. Your potential market consists of the core readers who you believe would faithfully turn to your column every time it appears. If you have room to describe your periphery readers in a sentence or two, do so. If not, focus solely on your core readership.

Here's how I might describe the core audience for my hypothetical column:

> *Simply Living* is a weekly 500-word column written for the millions seeking a more conscious, simple, healthy, earth-friendly lifestyle.

How can I say "millions"? If I applied the statistic used in my hook ("82 percent of eight hundred Americans agreed . . .") to the U.S. population, we would be talking about millions of people. Therefore, it's believable.

Also, note that I used the opportunity to include in the sentence the word count and frequency of the column. Inserting this information here saves space and provides the editor with additional facts about the column.

• *Pitch letters describe why your intended audience would want to read your column.* OK, so there is a market for your column, but why would they turn to you? In other words, what does your column offer them?

In my case, *Simply Living* would provide information for living a simpler life. Therefore, something as uncomplicated as this might suffice:

> This column offers fresh, practical and precise ways to live a life that is more healthy and rewarding.

If my column focused on products related to the "simplicity" movement, I could take this approach:

> Trends Research Institute predicts that by the year 2000, 15 percent of the nation's seventy-seven million baby boomers will be part

of a 'simplicity market' for low-priced, durable products. This column will direct them toward those products.

Without stating it outright, I've indicated to the editor that my column could draw advertisers seeking to sell these "low-priced, durable products." Those advertisers might include organic food producers and manufacturers of natural-fiber clothes.

If room permitted and I wanted to go the extra mile—and what aspiring columnist wouldn't?—I would contact those manufacturers, find out how much consumers spend on their products and how much that figure is expected to increase in the coming years. However, you may want to find these figures from a less biased source, such as an independent research firm. Finally, I would present these statistics to the editor.

If your proposed column competes with an established column that covers the same subject, mention it in your pitch letter. Certainly, there is no need to hide the fact that your column has competition. Chances are the editor to whom you're sending your letter is aware of the competition and will want to know how you intend to address it. So be forthright and tell her. Say my column competed against one called *Eco Guide*. Here's what I might write:

> *Simply Living* differs from *Eco Guide* in one very important way. Unlike *Eco Guide*, my column will share hands-on, real-life methods I have developed over ten years of working toward establishing a simpler life.

Notice I didn't describe what *Eco Guide* does. I don't have to, because the editor I send my pitch letter to will know. And since you have limited space in which to sell your idea, don't waste it telling the editor what she already knows.

• *The pitch letter describes how the column will fulfill readers' needs.* You've explained *who* would want to read your column and *why* they would want to read it. Now you want to explain *how* the column will accomplish what it has set out to do. Perhaps your column offers firsthand advice on how to close sales, or it offers your expertise on getting the most from your home computer. For my column, I might write something like this:

> By presenting amusing and insightful anecdotes based on my ten years of experience cutting out the clutter from my family's life,

Simply Living offers readers proven ways to live a life that is healthier and more rewarding.

Every column opens with a reader question, segueing into a response that includes an anecdote related to my experience. It then delves deeper into the issue by providing advice based on recently published material or interviews with experts. Finally, the column provides the results of a reader poll and concludes with a 'Winning Tip of the Week' for reducing waste. Both the poll and weekly tip are features available on my Web site.

- *The pitch letter explains how your column will assist readers.* Here, outline the benefits readers will gain from reading your column. For my column, I wrote:

People who have downshifted feel more in control of their lives and claim that their spending patterns are in closer harmony with their values, according to the authors of the book *Your Money or Your Life. Simply Living* readers can apply what they read directly and immediately to their own lives.

- *The pitch letter describes why you are qualified to write this column.* Remember, academic degrees and professional diplomas serve useful purposes in some cases, but don't feel inferior if you have neither. In fact, it could be a plus, as readers might identify more readily with you. To write a column about commuter gridlock, for example, you only have to have a driver's license.

In my hypothetical example, I would cite my ten years of experience downsizing. Perhaps I had published articles on the subject, or perhaps I wrote a book on the subject. Both amount to solid credentials in any editor's eye.

If your bio runs longer than a three-sentence paragraph, consider printing it on a separate sheet of paper. However, do not include extraneous information unrelated to the column just because you have the room to include it.

- *Finally, the pitch letter outlines your column's special features.* Ask *the Builder*, Tim Carter's column, is offered to newspapers free of charge. That's a special feature sure to catch the attention of any editor. Newspaper columnist Dave Lieber provides readers with a video version of his column on the Web site of the paper that runs the column, *The Fort Worth Star-Telegram*. Other features could include contests and reader surveys, both of which I've indicated were included in *Simply Living*. If you plan to write a column for the Web, a special feature could be hyperlinks to related sites.

Based on what I've written, here's how my pitch letter would look. To make it fit on one page, I had to tighten some areas and delete others.

Dear Ann Editor:

"Voluntary simplicity" is one of the major trends leading into the twenty-first century, according to the Trends Research Institute, which predicts that by the year 2000, 15 percent of the nation's seventy-seven million baby boomers will be part of a "simplicity market" for low-priced, durable products.

Simply Living is a weekly 500-word column written for the millions seeking a more conscious, simple, healthy, earth-friendly lifestyle. It is based on my ten years of experience cutting out the clutter from my family's life, and it offers proven ways to live a life that is healthier and more rewarding.

Simply Living opens with a reader question, segueing into a response that includes an anecdote related to my experience. It then delves deeper into the issue by providing advice based on recently published material and interviews with experts. Finally, the column provides the results of a reader poll and concludes with a "Winning Tip of the Week" for reducing waste. Both the poll and weekly tip are features available on my Web site.

Simply Living differs from *Eco Guide* in one very important way. Unlike *Eco Guide*, my column will share hands-on, real-life methods I have developed over ten years of working toward establishing a simpler life.

People who have downshifted feel more in control of their lives and claim that their spending patterns are in closer harmony with their values, according to the authors of the book *Your Money or Your Life*. *Simply Living* readers will be able to apply what they read directly and immediately to their own lives.

In addition to living what I preach, I have been profiled in *American Health* magazine and appeared on a national news program promoting my book, *Adapting a Simpler Life*.

I've included six sample columns for your review. I will call you in
three weeks to see if you're interested in *Simply Living*.
Sincerely,
Monica McCabe Cardoza

Like a column, a pitch letter is the result of lots of research and rewriting.
In fact, it's easy to become so consumed with its content that you never stop
tinkering with it. If that's the case, set it aside for a day or two, and when
you return to it, you may bring a fresh perspective that allows you to take
that all-important next step: Print it out and insert it along with six sample
columns into an envelope.

The Submission Dilemma

Submissions is one of those gray areas with which all writers eventually
have to deal—in particular, whether to submit your proposal to one editor
at a time or send it to several editors. A proposal submitted for consideration to more than one publishing company at the same time is known as a
"simultaneous submission" or "multiple submission."

Once taboo, multiple submission has become a fairly common practice
in publishing. If you plan to submit your work to a publication that won't
pay you more than a nominal fee, then it's acceptable to submit that piece
to more than one publication. And certainly, if you plan to submit your
columns to publications whose readerships do not overlap, it's acceptable
to do so simultaneously.

On the other hand, if your column could run in one of two competing
newspapers in your area, you may want to rethink a simultaneous submission. You may end up annoying the editors at both publications, who may
see your action as a way to pit the two editors against one another. In cases
such as this, send it first to the publication you most want to run it, and
in your pitch letter, explain that you're offering this newspaper the first
opportunity to run your column.

To speed up the approval process, attach a deadline to the proposal. It
could be a line at the end of your pitch letter: "I'll call you in three weeks
to answer any questions you may have regarding the column." Why three
weeks? I chose that amount of time because it's realistic. In today's workplace, two weeks feels like two days—any more time and the editor may
not remember your proposal. One note of caution, however: If you say
three weeks, make sure you contact the editor in three weeks—not two and

a half, not three and a half. Such a move proves to the editor that you're serious and can follow through on your promises.

Provide the editor with a self-addressed stamped envelope, commonly referred to by its acronym, SASE. An SASE is an envelope addressed to you, containing enough space and postage so an editor can return your piece if it's rejected.

However, just because you provided the SASE doesn't mean you may ever see it again. In a *Shop Talk at Thirty* column in *Editor & Publisher*, Chicago freelancer Margaret Carberry lamented the death of the tradition of editors returning unsolicited manuscripts to writers in SASEs. She wrote: "Don't they have any empathy for the poor, hopeful fool of a writer—any feeling about the cost and time involved in having to produce presentable new copy to try in another market?" Unfortunately, some editors don't.

You might consider including in your packet a self-addressed stamped postcard. The postcard, which you can create yourself on your computer, allows the editor to check one of several choices. For example: I'm interested and would like to speak with you; I'm interested, but unable to contact you at this time. Please call me in a month; I'm not interested now, but try me again in a few months; No, I'm not interested.

Such a gesture shows the editor that you value her time and increases the possibility that you will hear from her sooner. Finally, it indicates that you put a considerable amount of thought into your proposal.

❧

A well-executed submission strategy that takes into consideration basic submission etiquette, combined with a well-crafted, informative pitch letter, will convince an editor that your work is worthy of a serious, thoughtful review. In fact, your letter is not unlike one of your columns, which rewards readers with information or your special brand of advice. In the case of your letter, the reward for the editor is the opportunity to read your sample columns. Who knows? Perhaps your reward will be an acceptance call from the editor.

9 Where to From Here?

Your pitch letter packet has been sent to selected editors, and now you sit back and wait. Right? Wrong.

Now you start your follow-up regimen, creating a file of the editors to whom you sent packets and when the packets were sent. If you stated in your letter that you would contact the editor in three weeks, start a tickler file that alerts you to make that call in exactly three weeks—avoiding, of course, the weekend.

When you call, make the conversation brief. Leave a detailed message if you get voice mail: "My name is Monica McCabe Cardoza, and three weeks ago I mailed you a sample of my column, *Simply Living*. I said I would follow up in three weeks, so I'm calling to discuss how my column can generate new readers and advertising for your publication. I can be reached at (111) 555-1234."

Notice I expressed how my column could help the editor. This approach is more likely to spark the editor's interest than one where you gush about how badly you want to become a published columnist. Indeed, it's not enough to know how to write a column; a columnist should also be familiar with the business side of publishing.

If, after three weeks, the editor does not return your call and has not returned your material, you may still be in the running, or the editor may have no intention of returning your material, despite the fact that you provided an SASE. Call her, and if you have in mind another publication for your work, mention in her voice mail that you wish to submit your column to another periodical and would like to give the editor the first chance to accept it. If the editor has an E-mail address, try contacting her that way. Some people respond more quickly to E-mail than to phone messages.

If you don't have another publication in mind for your column, continue to call the editor, allowing a week between phone calls. But start to research other places that could run your column. Reconsider publications and Web sites that you originally dismissed. If you do not hear from the editor within two months of submitting your material, start to aggressively pursue other markets, chalking up your first attempt to experience.

Don't Give Up

Always present yourself as a professional, and don't get discouraged. Becoming a columnist is a long process—one that requires stamina and the ability to take rejection—so focus on maintaining a healthy perspective when it comes to placing your work.

If editors turn down your column, it may not be because they don't like it. It may have more to do with the realities of producing a periodical and making a profit. For an editor to publish your column in a print publication, a columnist may have to be dropped to make space for your column, or the newspaper will have to budget for increased space to run your work. (Even if you offer your work for free, the editor must find the space to run your column, leaving less space for paid advertising.)

If you want your work published on the Web, then space isn't an issue. However, payment may still be one. An editor may like your work but hedge at paying for it. In that case, consider allowing the online publication to run your column for free, with the idea that the exposure and credentials will give you the needed boost to get paid for your work and, if it's in your plan, to make it into print.

Editors, while wanting a fresh voice in their publications, often want a "name" as well, someone their readers will recognize as an authority in the field in which she writes. One way to build a name for yourself is to amass a collection of articles written by you on the subject of your column, or written by someone else, but featuring your quotes. You can then use these articles to sell yourself to editors. If editors ask you for published "clips," they are referring to these samples of your published work, usually clipped from the newspaper or magazine in which it appeared.

For columnists, clips enable them to get a foot in the door of additional editors. If one publication considers you good enough to publish in its periodical, it follows that other editors will give you a higher degree of consideration.

When collecting clips, make sure you preserve them neatly. Presenting an editor with a wrinkled strip of paper containing your words indicates that you may not have the neatest work habits. A writer with sloppy work habits is something no editor wants to get involved with. To that extent, consider pasting your column on a piece of paper, then when you send or present clips to an editor, make a photocopy of them. Indicate on the copy the title of the publication that ran the column, as well as the date it ran.

The only drawback to clips is that they represent the writer's work *after* it has been edited. As an editor, I know that the amount of work that goes into editing a column can be considerable. The published column is sometimes more the work of the editor than the writer. Therefore, you may be asked to supply "raw" copy of your work—that is, work that has not been edited.

A Household Name

While clips are strong selling points, they represent just one way to make a name for yourself. To build name recognition, consider these suggestions:

● Enter contests. Entering a writing contest says a lot about your devotion to your craft. It proves that you take column writing seriously enough to want to be recognized for it.

But before you say, "I never win those things," consider this: Winning a top prize is not as important as you would think. Even a secondary prize can be an excuse to send out a press release or add an impressive note to your background sheet (a one-page summary of your writing career and achievements). Try sending such a press release to the publications you have targeted as likely prospects for your column.

There are scores of writing contests and competitions held annually. To locate competitions, check out *Literary Market Place*, which has information on competitions and contests, as do the annual editions of *Writer's Market*.

In addition, *Editor & Publisher* magazine inserts an annual directory of journalism awards in its last issue of the year. The directory lists information on hundreds of awards, contests and scholarships available to journalists in all media, both national and international. It also lists contests suitable for columnists, including contests sponsored by the National Society of Newspaper Columnists, and the American Society of Business Press Editors.

Also, see if any associations or other organizations representing the field in which you write hold writing contests. Kansas City-based syndicated columnist David V. Chartrand wrote a column dealing with teen suicide that earned him the 1998 Media Award from the Mental Association of the Heartland, which represents mental health professionals from the Kansas City metropolitan area.

• Read your column on the air. National Public Radio will occasionally feature a newspaper columnist reading his latest column. If you're published locally and have written on a topic that would be of interest to listeners, approach the program director of your local radio station to see if she would be interested in having you read your column on the air.

• Write articles related to the topic of your column. One way to grow from a locally recognized expert to a nationally recognized expert is by getting your name in a publication seen by readers outside your locality.

If your column is about restoring antique cars, broaden the topic and propose it to a general-interest publication. For example, how about an article on an antique car museum for *The New York Times* Sunday travel section? If you write about child care, consider an article for *Parenting* magazine.

• Write an op-ed column. If the topic of your column lends itself to a newsworthy event, write about it in the form of an op-ed for a newspaper.

The Op-Ed page is usually placed opposite the newspaper's editorial page. Here, writers can respond to a newspaper's editorial, or they can write an original article on a subject with which they are concerned. In either case, they always receive "credit line" information—that is, their name and whatever "credentials" they would like shown are printed beneath their piece. A typical credit line might read, "Jane Smith, a columnist for the *Star-Ledger* newspaper."

• Start a personal Web site. The key to creating a site is to design it around content—think of your site as a resource. Readers are attracted to information, so ask yourself what sort of information you can provide that will draw visitors.

Post your columns, and offer useful information not found in them—perhaps information that did not fit into your published column. Offer to answer readers' questions, and provide links to other sites that may be of help to visitors. Self-syndicated humor columnist Tom Purcell uses his Web site (http://www.TomPurcell.com) to promote his column, and he offers more than eighty links for opinion editors. The links go to journalism organizations, trade journals, government bodies and major newspapers—a handy tool that draws opinion editors to the site, thus increasing the chances of them picking up his column for their publications.

Consider providing answers to readers' "frequently asked questions," often called FAQs on Web sites. For example, what are the ten most commonly asked questions about your subject area? Then provide an E-mail address and offer to answer questions personally. Post the most interesting questions and answers on your site.

Update your site periodically by adding new information and removing obsolete information or links. If your topic is in the news, provide coverage of "recent developments." Also, if applicable, post announcements of speaking engagements or conferences where you will be appearing.

Once your site is built, submit it to as many search engines and directories as possible. Do this by submitting directly to the major engines, such as Yahoo!, AltaVista, Excite, Infoseek, Magellan, etc. Each engine has easy-to-follow instructions on its home page for submitting your site information.

• Allow a newspaper to run your work for free on its Web site. At this point, most newspaper Web sites are not profitable, despite the fact that they get lots of traffic. If a newspaper editor expresses interest in your column, but offers the familiar phrase, "We don't have the money to buy it or the space to run it," consider offering the paper the right to run your column on its Web site for free. The exposure itself is terrific, and perhaps in lieu of pay, you can arrange for the paper to include a hyperlink to your Web site.

On the other hand, if your column runs in a publication that also has a Web site, offer the publisher the option of running the column for free on the site. Although the publisher may already feel entitled to do so, by making the offer, you may provide the necessary push to make it happen.

• Compile your columns into a book. Though at this point you probably won't have enough published columns to fill a book, start thinking about it. If you're writing a weekly column, it won't take long. Check out *Writer's Market* for book publishers specializing in your topic area, or consider finding an agent to represent you when the time comes. As with selling your column, both these tasks take time, so start early.

• Keep your eyes open for opportunity. When I was visiting the Web site of the National Society of Newspaper Columnists (http://www.columnists .com), I saw the headline "Computer columnist wanted." An "unidentified" newspaper was seeking someone to write a twice weekly 750-word column on computers and the Internet. The pay was fifteen dollars a column.

Acknowledging the low pay, the writer of the ad noted that he would consider material by someone who was already writing such a column. "That's an extra $390 a year for an E-mail message every two weeks," he wrote.

- Create a press kit. A press kit is nothing more than a dual-pocket folder containing such items as your profile, including awards won; your photo; and clips of your work. When the press calls seeking to do a story on you or the topic of your column, and they want to interview you as an expert, you'll be able to provide them with all the background material they need.

- Promote yourself on television. It's becoming increasingly important for writers to be able to present themselves to a viewing audience. Your local television station may welcome the opportunity to interview a local personality. In addition to the exposure, you can include a tape of your interview in your press kit. One syndicate, ParadigmTSA (www.paradigm-tsa.com), uses on its Web site streaming video segments of its columnists discussing their work.

- Check out writer's groups. In addition to providing support, encouragement and group discounts on items such as office supplies, some writer's groups hold seminars to keep their members abreast of the latest news related to their area of expertise. For example, Gallatin Writers, Inc. (Bozeman, Montana) consists of writers who examine local environmental conflicts plaguing the West, such as how to cope with the depletion of natural resources. Some of its members contribute to the Gallatin Writers' syndicated column, which appears in *The Seattle Times* and at least a dozen smaller newspapers throughout the West.

Setting Your Sights on Syndication

For some, writing a column is a hobby and having it placed in a local newspaper for little or no compensation is satisfaction enough. For others, a national publication is their focus and a three-figure payment per column is their goal. Still others aspire to be picked up by a large national syndicate, appear in at least one hundred newspapers and quit their day job.

From my discussions with syndicated columnists, it would appear that the majority of aspiring columnists seem intent on accomplishing the latter goal. Unfortunately, few writers grasp the realities of syndication.

One columnist I interviewed told me of an aspiring columnist who called her for advice. The caller wanted to syndicate a column targeted to Generation Xers. Unfortunately, she had not yet written even a single column and had no idea of the economic realities of syndication. Sure, some writers of nationally syndicated columns may earn fifty thousand dollars or more a year, but most syndicated columnists earn much less. That said, before you set your sights on syndication, understand what it is and how it works.

In general, syndication, whether done by the columnist or by a syndicate, involves selling a column simultaneously to different newspapers or magazines, usually for a commission on the sale price. Syndicated columns are promoted and sold to publications that pay for them according to the size of their circulation. The larger the circulation, the more the publication pays. However, according to one self-syndicated columnist, circulation has become a less reliable predictor of payment. She says some of her biggest newspaper clients pay less than some of her smaller newspaper clients. If this columnist was represented by a syndicate, it would take a commission of 40 to 60 percent of the net proceeds of the column (gross receipts less the cost of salespeople, promotion, mailing, etc.).

Self-Syndication

Self-syndication is the starting point for most columnists. It involves submitting completed pieces to editors at publications that do not compete with the one in which you're already published. If your local paper runs your column, you probably couldn't sell it to the competing paper, unless your editor gave you the OK, in which case there would probably be certain restrictions, such as the competing paper cannot run your column until after it has appeared in the first paper. In any case, before selling your column to other publications, run the idea by your editor, who can quickly tell you the ground rules for selling to other publications. Also, expect that other editors will want the same sort of exclusivity.

Beyond selecting suitable publications for your work, a self-syndicated columnist is also responsible for promoting and selling the column idea, establishing payment rates and billing publications. It's a lot of work, involving tasks seemingly unrelated to the reason you started writing columns in the first place. However, it ensures that the writer earns 100 percent of the proceeds.

Though self-syndication would seem a fairly straightforward endeavor, it's not. Jim Toler, a former United Media sales executive, opened his own syndicate, Toler Media Services, Fort Edward, New York, in 1997. In addition to representing six clients, including four columnists, he offers consulting for columnists interested in self-syndication.

Toler uses several criteria when considering whether to take on a consulting job: The columnist's material must be unique, it must fill a niche and it must be able to be localized. In addition, the columnist must have a fairly large ego. "A big part of my consulting is advising clients on various aspects of syndication, then turning them loose," says Toler. "They must be able to take rejection."

According to Toler, if a column is well written and meets the previous criteria, there is hope. "One thing you must make sure you're clear on is that this is not a get-rich-quick business," he says, "but a gut-grinding selling business."

One of Toler's clients echoes his sentiments. "It's a labor-intensive process," says self-syndicated columnist Azriela Jaffe. "It's basically a numbers game. I may be rejected nine times, but on the tenth time, I make a sale."

Jaffe, whose column, *Advice From A–Z*, offers guidance for the self-employed and home-based professional, says it's not necessarily what your column is about and whether it's well written—that's a given, she says. "It's about timing," she adds.

If you're lucky enough to get an editor on the phone, Jaffe recommends having a prepared description of your column that takes all of one minute to deliver, and delivering it in such a way that the editor knows you've done your homework. "You want to say something like: 'My name is Azriela Jaffe, and I'm known as the Ann Landers of the small business market. I write a small business column, and what's unique about it is that it focuses on the emotional and relationship concerns that small businesses have. I understand you have a Monday business section, and I believe my column would fit in well there.'"

She continues: "You don't want to say: 'I write a column, and everybody who reads it really loves it.'"

Jaffe adds that after three years of writing a column, she still needs to support herself with other freelance writing work. That's why she says you must think of column writing as a long-term process, one that may take as long as three to five years just to make a name for yourself.

Jaffe agrees with Toler's statement that columnists need to be able to take rejection. In fact, she feels it's so important that she's written a book on the topic: *Starting From "No": Ten Strategies to Overcome Your Fear of Rejection and Succeed in Business* (Upstart Publishing, 1999).

Beating the Odds

Aspiring to be picked up by a syndicate is a lofty goal, one that requires a tremendous amount of skill, timing, persistence and even luck. According to an October 3, 1998, article in *Editor & Publisher* magazine, the biggest syndicates receive seventy-five hundred to ten thousand submissions a year and sign fewer than ten of them.

Of the lucky few chosen for syndication, there's no guarantee it will last. Some syndicates are satisfied to have 50 percent of their new offerings stick around for at least five years. Sometimes the half-decade success rate is more like 30 percent. Columns are generally considered successful when they appear in twenty-five papers by their first anniversary.

Jim Toler explains that most large syndicates have systems in place to review column submissions and may acquire as many as one or two per quarter. Others may acquire far fewer. For example, the Washington Post Writers Group launched only about twenty features from 1990 to 1998, with about 75 percent of them still in syndication.

Syndicates that take on new columns often don't have the luxury of promoting them over the long term. According to one former salesperson, syndicate salespeople will push newspapers to carry the columns just taken on by the syndicate. But the next quarter, when one or two newer columns are taken on, the columns taken on the previous quarter get less promotion, and on and on until the columns selected the prior year hardly get a mention to editors.

One way to avoid becoming lost in the crowd is to hook up with a syndicate that specializes in a particular subject. If you write an automotive column, consider soliciting a syndicate that sells only columns about cars. Specialized syndicates tend to take on fewer columns than large newspaper syndicates and, therefore, can devote more attention to selling its columns.

If you think your column has international appeal, look for a syndicate that is involved overseas. Indeed, with fewer U.S. dailies, fewer multipaper markets (hence less bidding for columns) and smaller news holes, syndicates are going global, increasing international sales thanks in part to the Internet, which has made delivery to foreign papers easier and cheaper.

Syndicates are also selling more of their columns and features to online papers and other sites. While electronic sales represent the fastest-growing part of the syndicate business, in many cases syndicates charge online clients up to 80 percent less than print clients, reflecting the fact that many newspaper Web sites still are not profitable. However, considering that online sales constitute a business that barely existed six years ago, pursuing such a market now may ensure your success there later when these sites are making profits.

But newspaper Web sites aren't the only online entities buying columns. TV networks, radio stations, online magazines, associations and corporations are just a few of the other organizations with Web sites. These non-newspaper sites often have more revenue available for content and therefore tend to pay more for columns than newspaper Web sites.

Demand by non-newspaper Web sites for columns and other material is so strong that it has sparked the creation of companies syndicating exclusively to Web sites. One of these companies is iSyndicate, which delivers material to corporate, small business, e-commerce, media and other Web sites. Founded in 1996, the company amassed more than 17,500 clients just two years later. And while iSyndicate began by buying its columns from newspaper syndicates, as well as Web publishers and news services, it intends to eventually take on self-syndicated columnists. The company Web address is http://www.iSyndicate.com.

Despite a market that's dominated by ten big and many smaller syndicates selling columns to a decreasing number of newspapers with less space available for columns, more syndicates continue to open, finding creative ways to bring well-written, informative material to new readers. Such activity should spark optimism in aspiring columnists. Rather than viewing the market as in decline, columnists must see it for all its opportunities. Indeed, if you can look outside the traditional means of syndication, you will find entirely new opportunities.

10 Interviews With Columnists

Like a well-written column, the conclusion of this book brings readers full circle. Having discussed columns in all their specifics, here four columnists describe how they approach their craft.

Bob Rosner, *Working Wounded*

Bob Rosner likens business columns to castor oil—"They're good for you, but tough to get down." Having crossed the one hundred newspaper mark, with clients such as the *Los Angeles Times* and the *New York Daily News*, and writing more than two hundred columns, he has obviously found a formula for making business columns easy to digest.

Today, Rosner's 500-word advice column on managing job difficulties is also carried in *Costco Connection* and *Workforce* magazines, as well as on several Web sites, including his own (http://www.workingwounded.com); *The Wall Street Journal's* interactive edition (http://www.careers.wsj.com); Canada's *The Globe and Mail* newspaper (http://www.globecareers.com); ABC News (http://www.abcnews.com); and Yahoo! (http://www.yahoo .com). In fact, Rosner now earns more selling his column to Web sites than to newspapers.

Rosner is a commentator on National Pubic Radio and the author of *Working Wounded: Advice That Adds Insight to Injury*, a compilation of his columns (Warner, 1998).

How did you get your start in this business?

"About five or six years ago, I started reading business stuff and felt no one captured the craziness that was cracking in the workplace. So I wrote about thirteen columns, but they were never better than the stuff I was reading.

Then one weekend I was in the library and saw a book by [humor columnist] Dave Barry and started reading it. I wrote three columns that night.

"I brought the columns to a weekly newspaper in Seattle. I thought I wanted to become a writer for this paper and cover the business beat. The editor said, 'I'll give you $150 a week to write this column.' I had no idea this was a lot of money and was actually depressed because I wanted to be hired. He said, 'Bob, this is good stuff. Go and sell it.' I didn't realize he was setting up my business."

What happened after that?

"I went to two other newspapers. The people at a Tacoma, Washington, paper liked it so much they introduced me to a paper in Raleigh, North Carolina. I pitched four papers and got four yes's. Then I went to ten other papers around the country. I went 0 for 10. It was then that I realized how hard it was to sell a column.

"Around that time United Feature Syndicate called me. A sales guy in my region liked my column and took it to New York. They wanted to pick me up.

"At that point, I E-mailed ['Dilbert' creator] Scott Adams and said, 'Your syndicate wants to pick me up. What do you think?' He said, 'Don't hire just any lawyer. Syndicate law is very specific.' He suggested I use his attorney. I did that.

"I'm told there are three kinds of columnists: people with no newspapers; people who have three to five papers; and those with fifteen-plus papers. Syndicates take seriously those columnists with fifteen papers. Even though I was in the three-to-five paper group, I was walking in with an attorney they respected, and the sales guy felt my column was good, so they treated me well."

What advice do you have for aspiring columnists?

"You have to know the marketplace and realize that there are other people writing in the same area as you. Also, you can't make money in lots of little papers. And in the big papers, there are a lot of writers who wish they were columnists, and these writers are constantly looking for ideas to hang on a shingle. You need to reach a significant amount of readers, and you need a unique niche and voice, a defined market, and papers that don't have people who could write your column.

"If you want to go to a local paper with your topic, you have a good chance of being published if you're a good writer with a good niche. It could be run as an op-ed piece. If you want to get published on a regular basis in that paper, the odds are tougher. If you want to sell to other papers, the odds are worse.

"Syndicated columnists have two awful choices: Sell the column yourself and get anywhere from $50 to $150 for a column—but you will kill yourself knocking on all those doors—or go to a syndicate, and they will pay you $2 to $40 for that same column, based on the paper's circulation."

How do you generate ideas?

"E-mail. Thank God for E-mail and the ability it affords you to get in a dialogue with people.

"I also get about ten books per week from publishers and subscribe to or am 'comped' [given complimentary subscriptions to] business magazines, which allow me to stay on top of current business literature. I visit Web sites, and at every dinner party, I ask people what's bugging them. After hearing the same thing two or three times, I start to write a column."

What's the biggest challenge in writing your column?

"I have to be very focused to get everything into 500 words. The *Working Wounded* column consists of a letter and the column, plus a mix of other elements, including a 'List of the Week,' poll results from a reader survey I conduct and the winner of a contest I run. Every week, I challenge my readers to a contest. If someone can beat the advice I give on a particular topic, I give him one hundred dollars and a copy of my book.

"I also do a poll on abcnews.com every week. One of my favorite questions pertained to cubicle etiquette. I asked, 'Which Broadway show best expresses your feelings about working in a cubicle?' Sometimes I go after funny responses, sometimes I go after information."

How many letters do you receive from readers?

"I receive about one hundred letters a day and try to respond to them within forty-eight hours, but I might have to move that to seventy-two hours. I put my Web site address, E-mail address and fax number on every column to create a number of ways for people to get in touch with me.

"It's easy for a columnist to get into a mind-set that you're serving an amorphous mass, not human beings. You can forget why you got into the business, which is to have a dialogue with people. So I make answering my E-mail a priority." ❧

Tim Carter, *Ask the Builder*

Tim Carter may describe himself as "a guy who used to eat lunch on drywall buckets," but today, he's positioning himself to be the "Bill Gates of home-improvement columnists."

Since starting his 650-word self-syndicated column, in 1993, Carter has placed it in some ninety newspapers, and additional papers continue to pick it up. In fact, within twenty-four hours of interviewing him, two more papers had agreed to run his column.

In addition to finding a unique niche, Carter does what few columnists do—he gives away his work for free. As of January 1998, Carter stopped charging newspapers for his column; his existing customers pay, but Carter expects to eventually offer them the column for free, too.

Carter also hosts his *Ask the Builder* radio show, is the home-improvement expert on a local television station and runs a Web site that is featured in the book *StrikingItRich.com: Profiles of 23 Incredibly Successful Websites You've Probably Never Heard Of* by Jaclyn Easton (McGraw-Hill, 1998).

How is your column different from other home-improvement columns?

"There are a lot of columnists who write do-it-yourself columns, despite the fact that the majority of the population doesn't 'do it themselves.' They hire people to do it.

"I went down a separate road. I let the other columnists write about how to put up a fence. I write about how the fence *should* be put up. To my knowledge no one else is doing this—at least that's what editors tell me."

What makes you qualified to write such a column?

"I was a contractor for twenty years. I'm a master carpenter, a master plumber, a remodeler, and I always wanted to write a book on how people get screwed by contractors. Then I got a call from *The Cincinnati Enquirer*, which found out that I had won the 'Big 50' award from *Remodeling* magazine and wanted to do a story on me. I had no idea about the award. At the time, nominations were made secretly by manufacturers." (The Big 50 award is an annual award given to fifty industry leaders who excel in management, marketing, selling and design.)

"I met with a reporter from the paper, and we chatted, and the book subject came up, and she said that I should write it.

"Two months after getting the award, my wife said I should take my book idea and turn it into a newspaper column. So I went into my office and wrote six columns. I had the business card from the reporter who had interviewed me. So I took my columns, went to the paper and rode up the elevator, and she read two of the columns right there on the spot. She said she had to get clearance, but she wanted to buy them. She also said that I should sell them to other papers.

"I said, 'There's probably fifty other columnists out there just like me.' The reporter, Ann Haas, said, 'I've been in this business for twenty-five years, and every month we get calls from syndicates and proposals from independents like you, and I have never seen a column like yours.'

"I waited for tear sheets (samples of writing in its published form, cut from the newspaper or magazine in which it appeared), then went crazy sending them to papers. In one month, the *Chicago Tribune* bought my column. I went after the big papers. When I told Ann this, she said, 'You don't know what you've done. The *Chicago Tribune* doesn't buy from people like you.' "

Have you approached a syndicate with your column?
"I never went to a syndicate, because I run what's basically a mail-order business.

"I write a publication called *Builder Bulletin*, which contains more information than my 650-word column, including a resource list of manufacturers and their 800-numbers. I advertise it in a tag line at the end of my newspaper column. For three dollars, readers can get a copy. So I get all these envelopes with three dollars in them, and I pay for the return postage, mailing, label generation and data entry. I don't want any syndicate handling that part of my business."

How do you address the competition?
"I know there's someone else out there who's about a year away from doing what I'm doing. My job is to make it impossible for him, and anyone else, to get started.

"One of the ways I do that is by doing other things, such as recently publishing my first CD-ROM. It contains the truth about vinyl windows. It goes through the process of how homeowners should work with contractors and how they can identify quality windows. I sell it through my Web site, as well as to the manufacturers listed on the CD-ROM, and they're passing them out like candy to their potential customers."

How many letters does your column generate?

"I receive about five hundred *Builder Bulletin* orders, letters and E-mail each week, and that number is rising. My staff and I spend ten to fifteen minutes a day responding to letters.

"But I get far more E-mail questions than handwritten ones. Some I respond to with a complete answer; others I tag with a note saying I'm swamped and they can call me on my radio show."

Do you cover controversial topics?

"Yes. As a matter of fact, I'm writing a column now in which a couple of manufacturers are going to get creamed. They're fearful, and they've been calling me because they want to get their defenses up. I identified a problem with synthetic stucco. There are tens of thousands of homes that are rotting away due to this product."

What qualities make for a good columnist?

"Attention to detail. You also have to be prepared to work seven days a week and have hands-on experience on what you write about. I don't mean a person who bought one house, did minor rehabilitation work and now thinks he can write a column about it. I was in the trenches for twenty years. I wore a tool belt. I got hundreds of stitches. I was on roofs when it was 120 degrees. I did all the work, and that shows through in my writing.

"A columnist has to write columns that are real, that tell a story. No disrespect intended to journalists, and I almost failed English in high school, but I think journalists are taught to gather facts and report back. Columnists are different. People like to hear stories. My columns read a little like a story. To do that, you need to be creative and have experience."

What advice do you have for today's aspiring columnist?

"There is no money in this field. You have to be creative. I'm shocked at how newspapers have gotten away with paying a syndicated columnist so little. The average amount I get would not buy two people lunch." ❧

Dr. Scott Shalaway, *The Wild Side*

With a Ph.D. in wildlife ecology from Michigan State University and a home on ninety-five acres of woods in northern West Virginia, where he lives with his wife and two daughters, Dr. Scott Shalaway is in a unique position to cover all aspects of natural history—from birds and bats to outdoor travel and wildflowers—which he does in his weekly 650-word column.

Though *The Wild Side* covers a diverse range of topics, it has never strayed from its purpose: to educate and entertain readers so they can start to understand nature and, therefore, begin to care about it.

Where did your column first appear?

"In June 1986, it was picked up by the *Pittsburgh Press*, which has a circulation of 500,000.

"When I started writing a column, I didn't know anything about the business. I thought I'd write sample columns and send them out. At the last minute, I sent them to the *Pittsburgh Press*, and over the course of a month, they bought columns. It gave me instant credibility.

"They used it twice a month, then jumped to three times a month, then weekly. It's been running there every week since. Today, twenty-three papers run the column, and about one million people read my column every week."

Does your column generate letters?

"It generates a tremendous number of letters. Sometimes I'll write a column specifically to generate mail. I'll offer plans to build a nest box, and something like that can generate three hundred to eight hundred letters.

"Over the last six years, I've done a reader survey every other year posing twenty questions with multiple choice answers: Do you own a pair of binoculars? Do you travel to see wildlife? Last time, the survey generated over twelve hundred letters.

"I periodically copy a pack of twenty or thirty letters and send them to the appropriate editors in certain cities. Invariably they get back to me and remark on them.

"Since I went online about four years ago, I started getting E-mail. Since then the amount of correspondence I received has quadrupled. I've had a Web site for a year (http://www.shalaway.com)."

How do you respond to your competition?

"My column has broader appeal than other outdoor columns, most of which are based on hunting and fishing. Virtually 100 percent of the public has a passing interest in nature because they see butterflies and birds. So everybody is a potential reader.

"Furthermore, there aren't many people around with my background and experience. My competition is mainly local nature writers who have been writing about it for years in their local papers. They are part of a community and represent a market that I just can't crack."

What made you want to become a columnist?

"Before we lived in West Virginia, we lived in Oklahoma at Oklahoma State University. We didn't want to spend our careers in Oklahoma, because our families live in Pennsylvania, and also we wanted to own land. So we bought ninety-five acres in West Virginia and moved here in 1985.

"Once we got settled, there were a number of possibilities to generate income, and one was writing a nature column. At the time, I didn't know anything about popular writing or the newspaper business—and at the time, that was a great advantage. I muddled on blindly and got lucky.

"Once I got the *Pittsburgh Press*, that impressed others, and I got three or four papers in the first six months. I also had no experience in popular writing, but my wife writes for newspapers. I wrote three or four sample columns, and she rewrote them, so I essentially got a graduate course in nonfiction writing. She edited, criticized and worked hard, and slowly her influence rubbed off on me. It took me two to three years before I felt confident enough not to consult her."

Have you changed your column since you started writing it?

"When I first started, I wrote about 500 words. Now I write 650 to 700 words. It happened without me realizing it. If I turn in 600 words, I get calls from editors for more.

"Also, when I first started, it was a struggle to fill a page. Now when I sit down for one and a half hours, I write 650 words almost to the word.

"The focus hasn't really changed. The purpose of the column has always been to educate and entertain."

Who are your favorite nature writers?

"The best outdoor writer in the country is Steve Pollack, who writes for the *Toledo Blade*. I also love Ted Williams, who writes for *Audubon* and covers controversial topics. He's the best conservation writer. I've gotten to know them by joining writers' organizations and going to meetings."

111

Do you write about controversial topics in your column?

"Occasionally, no more than one or two a year. I've written about hunting, trapping and an annual pigeon shoot held in Harrisburg, Pennsylvania. The unspoken message I get from editors is they don't want me to do that—that it's better handled by their editorial people.

"Some controversial columns have not been picked up by newspapers, and others have been run on the editorial pages of the newspapers that carry the column. So I minimize it. Though I'd like to do it more, my purpose is to educate and entertain. Although topics I think are benign sometimes turn out to be controversial, and I'll get hate mail."

What advice can you give to aspiring columnists?

"Be persistent. Twenty-three papers sounds great, but I've been doing this for twelve years. I continue to go after papers, and my success rate is less than 10 percent, so you've got to accept the fact that people will say no.

"The biggest frustration is that editors will tell you they like your column, but they don't have the space or the money to run it. After two years in the business, I considered going to a syndicate, but they basically told me no one is interested in the topic."

Do you do anything else related to your column?

"I do speaking engagements, and I've published two books containing my columns: *The Wild Side* (1990) and *The Wild Side Volume 2* (1996).

"I also produce and host a radio show called *Birds & Nature*. I started that six years ago when I bought time with a local station and sold ads myself. It made money from the start. Now it's on satellite, and anybody can hear it. Five stations now carry it." ❦

Gene and Adele Malott, *The Mature Traveler*

Whether it's making a pilgrimage to Graceland or exploring the Bridge on the River Kwai in Thailand, Gene and Adele Malott are there to help mature travelers tour safely, cost-effectively and comfortably. Launched in 1991, *The Mature Traveler* provides information on travel discounts, destinations, packages, and experiences designed for people fifty years old and up.

Tell me about the columns you write.

"We publish a monthly newsletter, *The Mature Traveler*. All our work appears first in the newsletter. After we self-syndicated [the monthly column]

Get Up and Go to about a dozen senior publications, we were approached by The New York Times Syndication Sales Corporation to handle a weekly column for them. The Times distributes *The Mature Traveler* as part of its Way to Go Travel package each week to about forty daily newspapers throughout the world."

How did you break into column writing?

"We don't feel as though we 'broke' into column writing. It was a logical extension of our lifetime careers in journalism and of *The Mature Traveler* newsletter."

Do you get letters from readers?

"Yes. Sometimes we get as many as a couple of hundred a month via snail mail and E-mail. We answer them and use them in our column, but not as the exclusive content."

Did you always want to be a columnist?

"No, I [Adele] wanted to be a journalist. I wanted to be a journalist who knew a special subject thoroughly. That's usually the stuff a columnist is made of."

How has your column changed since you first started writing it?

"As the travel industry changes and mature travelers' interests change, so does our column. When we began the newsletter thirteen years ago, travel for seniors was a far different field than it is now. We did more in terms of exposing senior scams and educating readers on how to shop for travel."

How do you generate ideas for your column?

"The travel industry generates ideas. It is news-based."

Do you tackle controversial topics in your column?

"Sometimes. We initiated the publication of the cruise ship sanitation ratings and helped hold up the industry to public view in that regard. We have written repeatedly about travel scams, which can be considered controversial to advertisers. With the newspapers running the columns, we can only assume the editors appreciate it. Readers love it."

What qualities make for a good columnist?

"The sincere desire to be of help to readers." ❧

Following are the organizations and products mentioned throughout the book. Please note that some of these books are frequently available in local libraries.

For a fascinating look at column writing from its origins in the mid-1800s to the present day, check out *The American Newspaper Columnist* by Sam G. Riley, who self-syndicated his humor column, *Southern Whimsy*, from 1978 to 1981, and now teaches communications studies at Virginia Tech. The 272-page book is available from Praeger Publishers, Westport, Connecticut, (203) 226-3571.

Association of Alternative Newsweeklies

1660 L St. N.W., Suite 316
Washington, DC 20036
Phone: (202) 822-1955
http://www.aan.org
Visit this site to check out the "alts" in your area.

National Society of Newspaper Columnists

http://www.columnists.com
This is a great site for aspiring columnists. It tells who's writing what for which paper, details upcoming writing conferences and notes awards given to columnists.

It also publishes an annual booklet containing award-winning columns. As its Web site notes, it's a "wonderful study guide for columnists with big dreams." For order information, write NSNC Contest Booklet, P.O. Box 1203, Keller, TX 76244, or check out the society's Web site.

Newsletter Publishers Association

1501 Wilson Blvd.
Suite 509
Arlington, VA 22209
Phone: (800) 356-9302; (703) 527-2333
Fax: (703) 841-0629
http://www.newsletters.org
NPA's site contains listings of newsletters published by its members, which consist of publishers of subscription for-profit newsletters.

Newspaper Association of America
1921 Gallows Rd.
Suite 600
Vienna, VA 22182-3900
Phone: (703) 902-1600
Fax: (703) 917-0636
http://www.naa.org

This site offers the latest information on the newspaper industry, including the kind of material newspapers are using to attract readers.

Newspapers Online!
Phone: (608) 221-1131
Fax: (608) 223-1131
http://www.newspapers.com

This site allows users to find newspaper publications from around the world, including trade journals; specialty, state press, business and religious publications; and college and university newspapers.

Parenting Publications of America
Kathy Mittler, executive director
1846 Lockhill-Selma Rd., Suite 102
San Antonio, TX 78213
Phone: (210) 348-8396
Fax: (210) 348-8397
E-mail: parpubs@family.com

PPA consists of more than 150 publishers of regional parenting publications. Regular features in PPA publications include advice for parents on everything from prenatal care to teenage parties, information about outings, and reviews of plays, movies, books and local restaurants. Although it doesn't have its own Web site, you can learn about the readers of these publications, as well as the kinds of written material these publications run, by visiting http://family.go.com/Features/family_1997_05/dony/ppam/ppam.html.

Suburban Newspapers of America
401 N. Michigan Ave.
Chicago, IL 60611-4267
Phone: (312) 644-6610

Fax: (312) 527-6658

E-mail: sna@sba.com

http://www.suburban-news.org/

This association includes approximately 1,200 suburban newspapers in North America. Check out its Web site for information about community newspapers in your area and for the topics editors of these publications want to cover.

SRDS

1700 Higgins Rd.

Des Plaines, IL 60018-5605

Phone: (800) 851-SRDS (7737)

http://www.srds.com

SRDS publishes media rates and data for the advertising industry. Its publications contain detailed information on who reads particular publications, from business-to-business to consumer periodicals. Use this information to target the right publication for your column.

Editor & Publisher

11 West Nineteenth St.

New York, NY 10011

Phone: (212) 675-4380

Fax: (212) 929-1259

http://www.mediainfo.com

Editor & Publisher magazine is a weekly magazine covering the newspaper industry. Its "Syndicates/News Services" column reports on the latest columns being offered by syndicates.

Editor & Publisher Directory of Syndicated Services is an invaluable annual directory listing newspaper syndicates, columnists and columns arranged by subject category.

Editor & Publisher International Year Book is a three-volume reference set consisting of listings of daily and weekly U.S. newspapers (volume 1); U.S. and Canadian weekly, community, free, niche and alternative publications (volume 2); and names of editors at these publications (volume 3).

Gale Research Co.

P.O. Box 33477

Detroit, MI 48232-5477

Phone: (800) 877-GALE

Newsletters in Print contains descriptions of more than 11,500 newsletters published in print or online in the U.S. and Canada.

Encyclopedia of Associations: National Organizations of the U.S. contains information on nearly 23,000 nonprofit American membership organizations of national scope, including the purpose of the organization and the publications it publishes.

Gale Directory of Publications and Broadcast Media is a three-volume annual directory listing more than 35,000 newspapers and magazines in the U.S. and their circulations. The periodicals listed here are indexed according to subject and special interest.

F&W Publications

1507 Dana Ave.
Cincinnati, OH 45207
Phone: (513) 531-2690
Toll-free for subscriptions: (800) 333-0133

Writer's Digest magazine is a monthly magazine that covers the freelance writer's markets and will alert you to publications that may be suitable for your work, as well as offer helpful writing tips.

Writer's Market is an invaluable reference for aspiring columnists. This annual directory contains consumer magazines and trade, technical and professional journals. Best of all, it contains specific information as to what the editors of these publications look for.

One of the best features of this directory for columnists is the section within each publication that describes opportunities for freelancers to contribute columns.

Oxbridge Communications Inc.

150 Fifth Ave.
New York, NY 10011
Phone: (212) 741-0231; (800) 955-0231
E-mail: info@mediafinder.com
http://www.mediafinder.com

Oxbridge Directory of Newsletters includes more than 20,000 newsletters, loose-leaf publications, bulletins and fax letters.

The National Directory of Magazines provides information for more than 22,000 U.S. and Canadian publications.

The College Media Directory supplies information on more than 6,000 student and alumni newspapers, magazines, art/literary journals and year-books from more than 3,500 campuses.

The *Standard Periodical Directory* contains more than 75,000 U.S. and Canadian magazines, journals and newsletters. Includes house organs (company employee newsletters) and association publications. The annual publications are classified by subject.

INDEX

119